Praise for Alice Sink's Writing

I0798765

"Sink has taken her memories and channeled them into five years of research and writing that resulted in her book *The Grit Behind the Miracle*, which chronicles the true story of the Infantile Paralysis Hospital that was built in 54 hours in 1944."
—Jill Doss-Raines, *The Dispatch*

"Throughout the rare glimpses from 1900 to around the early 1950s, Sink stuck to one consistent theme in *Kernersville.* Sink portrayed the sense of community."
—Brandon Keel, *Kernersville News*

"*Boarding House Reach* reminds us of one of the most important truths of life: There are no ordinary people! Every story here is fascinating—and every one importantly belongs to history."
—Fred Chappell

"Community abounds in a colorful new book about the history of North Carolina boardinghouses—a traveler's guide to a lost place that was small town and worldly at the same time."
—Lorraine Ahearn, *Greensboro News & Record*

"A very highly recommended addition for academic and community library collections, *Boarding House Reach* could serve as a template for similar studies for other states."
—*Midwest Book Review*

"*Hidden History of the Piedmont Triad* recounts a number of interesting stories from throughout the Triad—from historic people and places to lesser-known colorful slices of life."
—Jimmy Tomlin, *High Point Enterprise*

"In *Hidden History of the Piedmont Triad*, Sink writes about Lexington's downtown dime stores. She describes how each counter was like a different department of the store, with a candy counter and comic book section popular with children…and makeup counters that carried old-fashioned items such as Tangee lipstick and Evening in Paris perfume."
—Vikki Broughton Hodges, The *Dispatch.*

"Did you know that a nightclub in High Point once hosted the likes of Ella Fitzgerald and Duke Ellington? Have you heard the story of Lexington native John Andrew Roman put to death on circumstantial evidence or the local World War II fighter plane pilot who flew eighty-two missions to prevent German fighters from attacking American bombers? These are but three of the many little-known stories…found in *Hidden History of the Piedmont Triad.*"
—*Arbor Lamplighter*

"*[Hidden History of the Piedmont Triad]*…covers people, places and events that have been forgotten."
Ryan Gay, lifestyles editor, *Kernersville News*

"In *Hidden History of the Piedmont Triad*, author Alice Sink rediscovers the quirky stories of the Piedmont Triad…tying North Carolina into the rest of world history."
—*Our State Magazine*

"*Hidden History of Hilton Head* offers a lively array of historical tidbits and tales. From beautiful poems written by renowned locals to the songs that guided the slaves to freedom and time-tested regional recipes, author Alice Sink's collection truly encompasses the spirit of the Lowcountry."
—The History Press (Charleston, SC)

"The premise of *No [Wo]man Is an Island* is outstanding! I laughed out loud—even hollered a few times…don't remember doing that since *Raney* and *Walking Across Egypt.* I can see it as a TV sitcom if the PC police wouldn't kill it."
—Carol Branard

"Thank you for *Hidden History of the Western North Carolina Mountains*—which is not really hidden. I knew almost all the stories and information and even some of the recipes. But then I'm supposed to, as an old Haywood County boy. Great to see it all in a book!"
—Fred Chappell

Wicked
Winston-Salem

Alice E. Sink

The History Press

Published by The History Press
Charleston, SC 29403
www.historypress.net

Copyright © 2011 by Alice Sink
All rights reserved

All images are courtesy of the Library of Congress.

First published 2011

Manufactured in the United States

ISBN 978.1.60949.458.2

Library of Congress Cataloging-in-Publication Data

Sink, Alice E.
Wicked Winston-Salem / Alice E. Sink.
p. cm.
Includes bibliographical references.
ISBN 978-1-60949-458-2
1. Crime--North Carolina--Winston-Salem--History--Anecdotes. 2. Corruption--North Carolina--Winston-Salem--History--Anecdotes. 3. Criminals--North Carolina--Winston-Salem--Biography--Anecdotes. 4. Winston-Salem (N.C.)--History--Anecdotes. 5. Winston-Salem (N.C.)--Social conditions--Anecdotes. 6. Winston-Salem (N.C.)--Moral conditions--Anecdotes. 7. Winston-Salem (N.C.)--Biography--Anecdotes. I. Title.
HV6795.W56S56 2011
364.109756'67--dc23
2011033502

Notice: The information in this book is true and complete to the best of our knowledge. It is offered without guarantee on the part of the author or The History Press. The author and The History Press disclaim all liability in connection with the use of this book.

All rights reserved. No part of this book may be reproduced or transmitted in any form whatsoever without prior written permission from the publisher except in the case of brief quotations embodied in critical articles and reviews.

Contents

Preface 9
Acknowledgements and Contributors 11

Part I. Public Concerns and Policies
Tobacco Warehouse Thieves 13
Slot Machine and Punch Boards 14
Whiskey Raids 14
A Major Nuisance Stuck in "Committee" 16
Wicked Smallpox and the Pesthouse 17
A Bad Impression 18
No, No and More No's 19
Epidemic of Spanish Flu 19
No Black Police Officers 19
Difficulties and Dangers for Salem 20
The "Lot" Determined Who Should Marry Whom 21

Part II. Crimes and Punishments
Guilty of First-Degree "Muddy Creek" Murder 25
The Ball Went Through His Heart 28
They Poisoned Their Daughters 28
Beaten into Unconsciousness and Critically Injured 29
The Frank Snipes Gang Successors 31
Libby Holman, Torch Singer, Accused of Murdering Millionaire Husband 32

Contents

Rape, Posse, Gunfire 36
The Drop Fell at 12:55—Broke His Neck 38
State Prison Escapee Recaptured after Twenty Years 40
Mob Storms Jail 41

Part III. Now You Know
He Claimed He Could Heal Anything—For a Price 45
Not in My Neighborhood 47
Lust for Fashionable Apparel 47
The Dreaded Invaders Arrived 49
Alderman "Blasted" Mayor 50
"Other Such Business" 51
Racially Tense Winston-Salem 53
At the Zinzendorf Hotel 54
Moravians in Salem "Going against Tradition" 56
Anything Wicked "Goes" for a News Snippet 60
He Said, She Said 64
"I Don't Want a Sterilize Operation" 69

Part IV. Believe It or Not
Board of Censors of Public Amusements 71
Salem Tavern—The Place to Drink, Argue, Duel 74
Obey Our Rules…Or Else 76
$10,000 in Currency Burned 78
Wickedly Heavy and Dirty Mill Work 78
Repeated Protests 80
No Unions! 82
Winston Officers Raid Distilleries 82
"They Take All the Pie" 83
Big Hudson Six Turns Over Three Times 84
Somebody Could Get Killed! 85

Part V. Straight from the Horse's Mouth
A Deplorable State of Affairs 87
Hand Over Your Money, or Else! 88
Sex in the Twin City 89
Joshua Coin—Blessing or Curse? 91
Suffering in Forsyth County—No Food, No Crops, No Money 92
The Greatest Catastrophe 95

"All We Ask Is to Be Let Alone"—Jefferson Davis 96
Fire Bugs 98
Racist Slogans and Ugly Epithets 99
Dispute Over Who Should Tax Tobacco 99
Infamous, Cowardly and Dastardly Attack 100
Cursing and Swearing on the Streets 101

Part VI. On the Lighter Side
First Court Case of Its Kind—The Butler Did It! 103
He Squealed on Daddy's Whiskey Stash 104
Ban the Wicked Circus? 105
Cigars and Tobacco Okay, but No Cigarettes on the Sabbath! 106
Circus Wagons Do Damage 107
Not on Sunday 107
Who Stole the $450? 108
It Was Just a Baseball Game! 108
How Dare You? 110
Five-Dollar Fines for Not Using "Soft Paper" 111
Relatives Need Not Apply 111
Wicked Arithmetic 111
Ordinances: Fire, Censorship and Whistling 112
Obey This Ordinance or Pay the Fine 113
No Weeds, Spitting, Loitering or Garbage in the Street 113
Winston Court Has Difficult Case 113
Thin, Puny and Lethargic 114
He Stole a Suitcase and Wore the Clothes 115
Strong Opposition to Sunday Movies 116
Halloween Celebration Canceled, but Dog Races OK 116

Appendix. Recipes Probably Served
in Old Winston and Old Salem 117
Bibliography 123
About the Author 127

Preface

Winston-Salem is one of my favorite cities. When I was a young girl, my aunt and I often rode the bus to the city of tall buildings and wonderful stores for a full day of shopping. We always ate lunch at the cafeteria beside the old bus station. One of my aunt's good friends worked at Sosnick's in the "better wear ladies' department." She always dressed in a business suit and pumps; her makeup and hairstyle were immaculate. For years and years, she attended to the needs of many wealthy women who shopped in "her" department. I suppose she was the first "personal shopper" I knew. I dreamed of one day having enough money to buy a prom dress at Sosnick's, but I—and my modest budget—always ended up at the Mother-Daughter Shoppe.

One of my daughters went to Salem College and later moved to Winston-Salem with her husband. Three of my grandchildren were born in Forsyth Hospital. My husband, Tom, and I attend church at Green Street United Methodist Church in that city.

For many years, in the 1980s and early 1990s, I taught in the Continuing Education Department of High Point College (University) at R.J. Reynolds Tobacco World Headquarters and also at Davis Training Center at Piedmont Airlines in Winston-Salem. In addition, I taught business correspondence courses for Piedmont Airlines employees.

So, I have good memories of Winston-Salem. Today, I present programs and have book signings for Winston-Salem businesses and book and civic clubs. My personal perception of the city is positive; however, as is the case in all places, history does sometimes rear its wicked little head, and when it does, chilling—but true—stories are revealed.

I think it is extremely important to reconnect with the various dictionary definitions of "wicked":

> *Morally bad or wrong; acting or done with evil intent; depraved; iniquitous; Generally bad, painful, unpleasant, etc., but without any moral considerations involved (a wicked blow on the head); Naughty in a playful way; mischievous; Slang: Showing great skill (he plays a wicked game of golf).*
>
> —Webster's New World Dictionary, *Second College Edition*

This book is dedicated to "Yar." For our friend who doesn't have a wicked bone in her body—a Winston-Salem resident who has helped right many of the wrongs.

Acknowledgements and Contributors

Once again, many thanks to my husband, Tom, who continues to offer suggestions, proofread my manuscripts and graciously "drive Miss Daisy" (as he calls his chauffeuring) to presentations and book signings. I truly appreciate my History Press editor, Jessica Berzon, who always kept me headed on the right track while I was researching and writing this book. Her editorial advice is priceless. Katie Parry and Dan Watson, my publicists, work diligently to arrange presentations and book signings, and I sincerely appreciate their continued efforts and publicity. A big thank-you to Jaime Muehl, senior editor, who keeps me on track with Chicago (15th edition), house deviations, spelling and consistency. As for Jamie Brooke Barreto, sales specialist, let me assure you that her marketing skills are superior, and for that talent, I am grateful.

For the High Point University Smith Library folks who helped me find necessary research materials through Interlibrary Loan and helped me access places on the Web that I never dreamed were there, thank you! David, Mike, Bob and Nita—you never ran away when you saw me entering the library!

I also wish to acknowledge all those real southern folks who, unbeknownst to them, gave me inspiration, ideas, tidbits and specifics concerning *Wicked Winston-Salem*.

Finally, on another positive note, I want to thank all those Winston-Salem people who, through great efforts, patience and sacrifice, helped "right the wrongs."

Part I

Public Concerns and Policies

Tobacco Warehouse Thieves

The robbers were called an "organized band of tobacco thieves" in a December 12, 1927 newspaper article entitled "Tobacco Thieves Have Been Active at Winston-Salem." Warehouse officials and Winston-Salem police officers arrested a man alleged to have been attempting to cash tickets for stolen tobacco. Following are the details:

> *Many piles of weed in some of the warehouses are said to have disappeared after being bought and it is believed thieves turned the tickets, removed the piles, and cashed the tickets upon resale. One warehouse is said to estimate that $1,000 worth of tobacco was stolen there and another is reported to estimate $800. One farmer is said to have lost his truck and a load of tobacco, which was parked outside a Winston-Salem warehouse. It has not been learned whether he recovered any of his property.*

Officers reported that a week earlier, they found an abandoned Ford on a highway in Forsyth County, with empty tobacco sacks in it and evidence that tobacco leaves had also been there but were now gone.

SLOT MACHINE AND PUNCH BOARDS

Belvin Miller, an employee of the Veterans Administration office in Winston-Salem, discovered that there is truth in the old saying "Three Strikes and You're Out." He had an automobile accident, and when officers answered the call, they found unlawful lottery equipment in his vehicle. When his case went to court, his reckless driving case was dismissed, but he was given a six-month suspended sentence and fined $250, plus court costs. What was Mr. Miller's story? According to a newspaper account:

> *He was quoted as testifying that the slot machine belonged to a friend who kept it in his basement for amusement and that he, Miller, was taking it to have it repaired. He was also said to have testified that the punch boards belonged to a friend who operates a service station and who was sending them back by Miller.*

WHISKEY RAIDS

Sidney Mize, in trouble at Winston-Salem "on account of alleged dealings in whiskey," also had a federal case against him for "figuring in a sensational scrap" at nearby Welcome, North Carolina. The August 22, 1921 newspaper account relates that Mize was under $800 bond after his moonshine still, the "tin lizard" kind, was destroyed by officers, who also confiscated and destroyed two kegs "containing between seven and eight gallons of whiskey, a hundred gallons of beer and two gallons of low wine." The story of the raid does have a humorous twist:

> *Mize and his partner were captured as they were coming away from the still, each carrying a keg on his shoulder partly filled with liquor. The officers arrived near the still just as operations were ending for the evening and saw a lantern moving through the undergrowth near the place. Deputies followed the lantern and soon gained on the men bearing the kegs. Becoming weary they sat down their burdens and rested on the ends of the kegs. The officers made a dive and grabbed the two men. Mize made no struggle, but the other man, being of powerful stature and also being very badly scared, let out a curdling yell and scuffled with one of the deputies. They had a fierce shuffle, until finally the prisoner slipped from the grasp of the officers and darted away in the darkness.*

Above: Two men of the U.S. Internal Revenue Bureau carrying packages of confiscated liquor.

Below: Man carrying confiscated liquor.

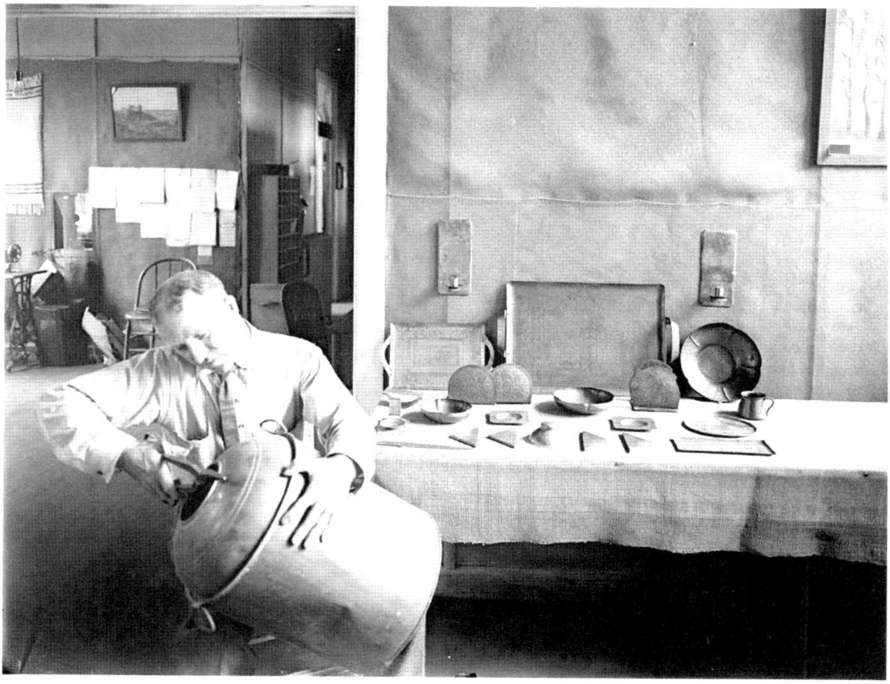

Policeman standing alongside a wrecked car and cases of moonshine.

Officers took Mize to jail and then went to the home of the second man, whom they had recognized after he lost his hat during the raid; however, he was not at home.

A MAJOR NUISANCE STUCK IN "COMMITTEE"

The City of Winston-Salem government meeting notes for July 4, 1913, addressed a complaint about sewage in Salem Creek. It appeared that property owners on Salem Creek had asked the board to "appoint a special committee to meet with the land owners affected by sewerage pipes emptying into the creek, and to examine the conditions which are now in existence," find a way to remove what was there and find methods to keep this from happening again and again. The minutes read:

> *Complaints such as this are not new. Winston Aldermen heard such complaints some 10 years earlier and referred them to committee. These sewers had been built over 30 years ago with disposal at this point. With*

A mechanical digger opening a sewer line.

> *the continuing growth of the town, it was obvious that this condition was not creating a major nuisance.*

Wicked Smallpox and the Pesthouse

According to the *Book of Minutes* of Winston's board of aldermen, the first day of January 1882, a smallpox epidemic swept through the town. The board issued an edict that everyone—young and old—receive a smallpox vaccination. For those already ill with the disease or individuals having been exposed to someone with smallpox, a pesthouse opened to quarantine—under guard—those persons. The cost of the pesthouse rental was four dollars a month. The following minutes are from a meeting of the board called on January 14, 1882:

> *Whereas it appears that the persons confined in quarantine in Winston on account of having been exposed to smallpox have become drunk and are threatening to break the grounds and spread the disease, one motion ordered that persons confined within the limits of quarantine who shall become disorderly shall be punished by having a ball and chain put on them.*

Five days later, the board of aldermen issued another edict that prevented anyone from entering Winston from the NWNC Railroad "without first being vaccinated or presenting satisfactory proof of vaccination to the physician in charge at the Depot." A smallpox epidemic was not a new concern for the area; in April 1779, a soldier had arrived with the disease, causing Salem to experience panic for the next six months.

On January 15, 1900, the Town of Winston Directing Board spent a great deal of time talking about the smallpox epidemic in Forsyth County because, according to the city attorney, "this City is in great danger and steps should be taken at once. A system of quarantine could be made practical and the only sure preventative was vaccination." Minutes show that the following discussion ensued:

> *The Aldermen agreed that public sentiment did not favor compulsory vaccination and suggested that action be deferred until a mass meeting of the town was called to fully discuss the "dreadful effects of an epidemic of small pox." 2000 circulars were printed for a meeting to be held the next night at the courthouse.*

Two days later, on January 17, the board again met because the vaccination ordinance had been unanimously approved at the town meeting. An ordinance was enacted "requiring all citizens to be vaccinated within 10 days. If a person was unable to pay, the City would absorb the expense." Less than a week after that, a case of smallpox "was confirmed in a room in the Gray Block. The superintendent of health recommended that...the patient be removed to the small pox hospital and also send to the detention house all persons exposed to the disease by reason of visiting the room." This detention facility was called a pesthouse and was located on the outskirts of Winston.

A BAD IMPRESSION

On February 2, 1902, the board of aldermen of the city of Winston made this unanimous resolution:

> *Resolved...the Southern Passenger Depot is not in keeping with the enterprise and progress of our City in that it gives to visitors a wrong impression of our town, that it is totally insufficient to give necessary*

comfort and convenience to the traveling public. It is also the opinion of this Board that the immense revenue derived by the Southern Railway Company from the business transacted at this point, entitles the Citizens of Winston-Salem to a large, convenient and comfortable Passenger Station.

No, No and More No's

At the October 20, 1914 board meeting, members approved the following ordinances relating to the fire department: "NO—interfering with the Fire Department, giving a false alarm, driving over a fire hose, interfering with fire prevention rules and drinking alcoholic beverages in a fire station."

Epidemic of Spanish Flu

On October 5, 1918, the U.S. Health Service made the following important announcement:

The City was ordered to close all public gathering places, schools, churches, theaters, picture show, etc. on account of the epidemic of Spanish Influenza. It was agreed that the City had no other course of action since in effect the State Board of Health had prohibited all public gatherings. Clippings from newspapers from a number of North Carolina cities were read showing that such action had already been taken in the larger cities. The matter was left in the hands of the Health Committee with power to act.

No Black Police Officers

The minutes of the March 7, 1919 Winston-Salem Directing Board indicate that a group led by F.M. Fitch, a prominent African American businessman, appeared before the board to suggest the following implementation:

If it was possible to secure one or two colored men, of the right type, and give them authority of an officer to work among the colored people only, he felt they might be able to ferret out crime that it would be impossible for a white officer to do. The Mayor referred the request to

> *the Police Committee and assured the colored people that it would be given serious consideration of the committee.*

According to reports, no black police officers were hired until 1943.

DIFFICULTIES AND DANGERS FOR SALEM

In her article "Around Salem Square," Adelaide L. Fries focuses on the difficulties and dangers that befell Salem in 1780. She writes about losses in both trade and handicrafts, the falling currency, extremely high taxes and the "constant demand for grain and cattle for the troops." In addition, residents were always willing to help those poverty-stricken families who passed through Salem, "though it increased the burden on the slender resources of the town." By 1781, Salem experienced more problems:

Major General Nathaniel Green.

> The war approached nearer and nearer to Salem. First came parts of Greene's army: ammunition wagons, which stopped to load shells, and the field hospital, which stayed only one day but left behind the more seriously wounded men to be cared for by the Salem doctor, Jacob Bonn. Then came lawless militia, and the Wilkes men especially seemed to delight in excesses of every kind, including personal attacks.

According to historian Fries, things got worse. Lord Cornwallis and his army

Surrender of Lord Cornwallis.

arrived at Salem, "making demands; the camp followers stole a great deal." The next few days were fairly quiet, but the days from the fifteenth to the eighteenth were "days of darkness and terror." Salem homes and businesses were plundered, and residents were assaulted. Citizens were happy to learn of the Preliminary Treaty of Peace, which was signed in Paris on January 20, 1783. When the news finally reached Salem on April 19, Moravians planned a Day of Thanksgiving for July 4, 1783.

The "Lot" Determined Who Should Marry Whom

William K. Hoyt, who presented a paper entitled "The Lot, the Youth and the Schobers" to the Winston-Salem Torch Club, explores the Moravian procedure of submitting a question to the Lord by using the "Lot." Just what was the significance of the Lot? An explanation follows:

> *Members of the Elders Conference gathered at a small wooden bowl containing three reeds: one marked Ja ("Yes"); one marked Nein ("No"); the third, a blank. Prayerfully the question was asked and a reed drawn. If the Ja or Nein reed was drawn, the "Yes" or the ""No" was accepted as the Lord's answer to the question. If the blank reed was drawn, it was*

> *taken to mean that the question was not properly stated, was prematurely asked or should not have been asked at all.*

So what does the Lot have to do with marriage? According to Hoyt, "If a man wished to marry, he was not allowed to propose marriage to the girl of his choice. Instead, he submitted her name and his ambition to the Elders." This is what transpired next:

> *If the proposed marriage conformed to the rules of the congregation, the question was referred to the Savior through the Lot. If He approved, the proposal was made in the man's behalf by the Elders to the girl or to her parents. She or they were at liberty to accept or reject the offer. If the Savior disapproved, there was no appeal.*

Apparently, not everyone obeyed the rules, because according to Hoyt, "early in 1774, a Single Brother in Salem became engaged to a young woman in Bethania without consulting the officers of his choir or the congregation." Trouble ensued both in Bethania and in Salem. Eventually, two of the prospective groom's friends loudly objected to the engagement procedures required by the elders; they were accused of insubordination and banned from the village. Other incidents indicate that proposals for marriage were not simply between a man and a woman but also the ruling elders. Such was the case of the 1774 incident when a single sister became engaged to a widower. She was "dismissed from the choir house but was chaperoned to be married by a Justice of the Peace." Then there is the following February 3, 1778 incident:

> *Salem's Elders Conference considered the household difficulties of Br. Jacob Kapp, who operated two mills near Bethabara. He had been a widower for a year, had four small children and only a stupid maid to look after his household. The Conference thought he should marry again, and suggested a widow, Johanna Elisabeth Steinmann. The Lot approved but she declined. In July, "the situation of poor Br. Knapp was again mentioned," and it was decided that another widow, Christina Dixon, should be considered for him. The Lot approved but he declined. The following March, Marc Hohns of Friedberg declined the proposal that his daughter should marry Br. Kapp. Finally, in May, Kapp got Sr. Elisabeth Everit of Salem as his wife and housekeeper.*

Home Moravian Church, Winston-Salem.

And the Lot saga concerning marriage continued when, in 1809, Johanna Sophia, known for her "spirit of non-conformity and independence," became engaged—without benefit of the Lot—to Van Neman Zevely. The events following their non-sanctioned engagement were as follows:

Bethabara Moravian Church, Winston-Salem.

> *Convinced that the marriage could not be prevented, the Elders decided on August 30 that the prospective bride and bridegroom could be considered* auswartige *members. Whereupon the* Aufseher Collegium, *which mainly concerned itself with temporal maters, sprang into action. Unanimously it ruled that if the marriage took place, the congregation boards should have nothing to do with it. The Elders Conference then decided that it could not "refuse to support the Collegium." So Gottlieb was notified that if the marriage took place, Johanna Sophia and Van Nemen would be considered to have left the congregation.*

True love prevailed, so the two were married and relocated. The following year, they sought "approval of the Lot and were re-admitted to the Salem Congregation." Interestingly, they could not move back to Salem; however, records indicate that they "maintained cordial and cooperative relations with the Brethren."

Part II
Crimes and Punishments

Guilty of First-Degree "Muddy Creek" Murder

The date was August 11, 1915. The caption read: "Two Sentenced to Death: Ida Ball Warren and S.P. Christy Convicted of Murdering G.J. Warren." According to the news article, the jury rendered a guilty verdict shortly before midnight on Saturday. Mrs. Warren and Mr. Christy were both sentenced to death in the electric chair. A third person, Clifton Stonestreet, son-in-law of Mrs. Warren, was given three years in the state prison. Following are details concerning the trial:

> *Judge Cline in sentencing the woman and the man to death fixed September 24 as the date for the execution. The trial of what is known as the "Muddy Creek Murder Mystery" cases came to a close Saturday night at 8:45 o'clock with the completion of Judge Cline's charge to the jury. The closing argument for the state was made by Solicitor Graves who concluded at 6:25. Judge Cline immediately began charging the jury, finishing his charge at 8:40. There was no adjournment for supper and immediately after receiving the case the jury retired to the hotel for supper and afterwards began making up its verdict.*

It seems that "late-night" court continued, with the jury reaching its verdict after 11:00 p.m. and being polled about 11:50 p.m. Judge Cline

"The Drama of the Criminal Court."

pronounced the death sentence for Mrs. Warren and Christy. According to the report, "His honor was visibly affected as he asked the prisoners to rise." Then Judge Cline "authorized the entry of a notice of appeal from this judgment to the Supreme Court. Why was Clifton Stonestreet spared the death sentence? The verdict against him was "guilty as an accessory after the fact and the court pronounced a sentence of three years in the state prison" for him.

How did those accused act? The news article gives the following specific details:

> *The prisoners stood calmly during the entire ordeal of their sentence; not once did Christy appear to weaken. Mrs. Warren stood erect during the progress of the court's address and sentence until the final words setting the date upon which they are to go to the death chair was reached. It was then that she quivered; shifted on the feet and as his honor concluded with "May God have mercy on your soul, be seated," she turned with a quick nervous jerk and sank into her chair. For a moment her head dropped and then she resumed her apparent calm.*

The town clock struck twelve o'clock midnight. The trial was over; however, not everyone left the courtroom. Even the prisoners stayed, conversing with

Electrocution.

each other and with their counsel. One of the "distinguished jurists" also stayed and made this statement:

> *In the event Mrs. Warren was sent to the chair, it would not only be the first woman electrocuted in the state, but the first white woman and the second woman to pay the death penalty. The only other woman was a negress, who was hanged in 1883.*

Only at the close of the news article do readers discover why the case was called "Muddy Creek Murder Mystery":

> *Warren was missed from his home in Winston-Salem after August 18 of last year and his body was found in Muddy Creek, Forsyth County last April. Christy, during the interim had gone back to Texas, where he had lived for years with Mrs. Warren, when the woman, then posing as the wife of Christy, alias Kearns, eloped with Warren.*
>
> *Mrs. Warren, arrested after the discovery of the body, according to the police, made a confession implicating Christy, who was extradited. Christy is then said to have made a confession in which he told of a plot by him and Mrs. Warren to kill her husband.*

THE BALL WENT THROUGH HIS HEART

"Homicide at Salem" was the caption of a February 24, 1904 article that reported "a mysterious homicide committed in Salem." Sidney Disher, age twenty-one, was shot by an unknown party, and "the ball went through his heart."

Police searched diligently for the Negro suspected of killing Disher; however, they were unable to find him. Consequently, the three white men—Tom Munday, Ralph Sanders and Milton Brewer—who were with Disher at the time of the shooting were arrested and jailed until an investigation could be conducted by the coroner. Following is news from the coroner's inquest:

> *The three white men claimed that a negro had fired the shot which killed Disher. Later they were substantiated in their statements by the arrest of Crawford Boyd, colored, aged 55 years, who confessed that he shot Disher. In his evidence, Boyd claims that Disher was trying to throw him over an embankment while Brewer, one of Disher's friends, was making at him with a knife when he fired.*

After Boyd's confession, the three white men were released, and Boyd was scheduled to be tried at the present term of Superior Court.

THEY POISONED THEIR DAUGHTERS

The May 24, 1928 front-page caption read: "Winston-Salem Couple Held for Poisoning Girls." The guilty couple was Herbert E. Hall and his wife, Laura Grace Hall, and they were placed in jail at Winston-Salem on the charge of first-degree murder "growing out of the death of two small daughters of Hall, step-daughters of Mrs. Hall." It first appeared that the girls had died of ptomaine poisoning following a dinner of sardines; therefore, the coroner's jury found no reason to indict a double murder. This is what happened to change the verdict:

> *Word of the death of the children from "ptomaine poisoning" reached officials of the National Canners Association through press dispatches and they immediately sent representatives to Winston-Salem who asked that further investigation be made. The corner ordered the bodies exhumed and the stomachs were subjected to a careful examination. Dr. T.C. Redfern,*

The age of drugs.

> *who conducted the autopsy, stated that he found enough arsenic in the stomachs to have killed the entire Hall family, which included four other children. This evidence was presented to the Forsyth grand jury, which was in session, and true bills charging murder were returned against the father and step-mother of the little girls. They are now in jail.*

Upon further investigation, authorities learned that Mr. Hall had asked for welfare assistance several times, saying that he had lost his former farm because of a "defective deed." After his daughters' deaths, he asked Forsyth County to pay their burial expenses. In addition, authorities discovered that Hall had filed for insurance in the amount of $2,030 on the lives of the dead girls. The article emphatically states that payment was being withheld pending further developments in the case.

Beaten into Unconsciousness and Critically Injured

On June 17, 1950, a front-page newspaper article entitled "Mauled Winston-Salem Girl Hovers Near Death" related the beating of seventeen-year-old Betty Jane Clifton, daughter of Thomas E. Clifton. The report indicated that Betty Jane had been taken to City Memorial Hospital in Winston-

Salem, where a "weary detective and her anxious family were keeping vigil outside the door." These events preceded her hospitalization:

> *Betty Jane was found at noon yesterday by her father when he went to his radio shop, beaten into unconsciousness and critically injured. Meanwhile Winston-Salem's entire detective force is securing the downtown neighborhood of the attack. Several fruitless leads have been followed, but no arrests have been made as yet. The case is described as one of the more baffling in Winston-Salem in years.*
>
> *The young girl, whose ambition was to be a nurse, is still unable to name the savage fiend who attacked her. Doctors found outward indication of an attempt at rape, they told the police, but have been unable to perform complete examinations which would reveal the full extent of the assault. They were more concerned with saving Betty Jane's life. Her face is battered to a pulp, with one ear almost severed, her jaw is fractured and there is a skull injury with possible fracture.*
>
> *She has been given numerous transfusions and is in an oxygen tent, having been removed only a short time for X-rays.*

A very bad man.

A little over a week later, another article appeared. This time, the caption read, "Negro Admits He Assaulted Girl in Winston-Salem: Girl Still Unconscious; Negro Denies Rape, But Rape Warrant Is Issued."

Clyde Brown, age nineteen, confessed that he had beat Betty Jane Clifton with a rifle in her father's Winston-Salem store because the girl discovered him trying to steal money from the cash drawer. Brown denied that he raped the young woman. A hearing for Brown was delayed until Betty Jane regained consciousness and was well enough to testify. Doctors feared she "may have sustained a permanent brain injury"; however, "she had moaned several times when her name was called."

The Frank Snipes Gang Successors

Several robberies had been committed in the Twin Cities and surrounding smaller towns—Welcome, Kernersville and Lexington. The newspaper article on December 19, 1921, entitled "Robbers Held at Winston-Salem Are Wanted Here" gives interesting details of Ray Huffman and Charles Huffman, arrested after they allegedly attempted to blow the safe of the Bank of Kernersville and also rob A.M. Ripple's safe at the Welcome Milling Company. Interestingly, one of those men arrested by Forsyth deputies and Winston-Salem police was wearing an overcoat belonging to Mr. Ripple, stolen the same night as the robbery. They are believed to be the same parties who also attempted to get into the safe in Woodrow McKay's Lexington garage the same night as the Welcome robbery. The Bank of Kernersville robbery attempt was reported by Mrs. Dewey Musten, a night telephone operator who was in the exchange over the bank:

> *Mrs. Musten heard someone making an attempt to gain the interior of the banking house. She telephoned the mayor and police chief and it is believed the would-be robbers heard her, got into their car and fled toward Winston-Salem. The plucky operator quickly called Winston-Salem and had officers sent to meet the car. A Kernersville police organized immediately and took the trail, coming up with the Huffmans and two companions, Grady Cheek and J.D. Cardwell, just after they had been arrested by Forsyth officers. The automobile tires were tracked from Kernersville.*

When he was arrested, one of the men, Roy Huffman, had nitroglycerin, fuses and dynamite caps in his possession.

Bank robbery.

The newspaper article concludes with general information concerning Twin Cities robberies:

> *This is not the first time that robberies committed...have been traced to thugs who hung around the outskirts of Winston-Salem, and it has been suspected that other crimes committed...had their origin with the same band. Several big house robberies have recently been committed in the Twin City and it is considered probably that some of these and a long chain of other crimes may be traced to the four men now in jail. They seem to be successors to the Frank Snipes gang, which did some store breaking jobs at Welcome and other places.*

LIBBY HOLMAN, TORCH SINGER, ACCUSED OF MURDERING MILLIONAIRE HUSBAND

According to author Milt Machlin in his book entitled *Libby*, "Libby Holman was the first of the torch singers, a Broadway star whose sultry, honeyed voice was likened to a *purple flame* when she sang the blues. Not remarkably beautiful, she possessed an allure irresistible to both men and women, and numbered among her lovers Tallulah Bankhead, Jeanne Eagels and Montgomery Cliff."

The back cover of Machlin's book reads, "Her marriage to millionaire playboy Smith Reynolds was front-page news. Scant months later, a bullet ended Reynolds' life on his fabulous thousand-acre estate in North Carolina. Although Libby was accused of Reynolds' murder, no conclusion was ever reached. Even her closest friends were divided as to her innocence or guilt." These excerpts from Machlin's book attempt to relive the night of that fatal accident:

> *The guests who trooped into the palatial Reynolda living room on Tuesday, July 5, comprised a fairly typical cross-section of Winston-Salem's younger life…Essentially it was a small, intimate group of Smith's friends plus Libby's friend, Blanche Yurka, who was seventeen years older than Libby and about twenty-five years older than most of the guests.*
>
> *How much drinking was done at the party later became a matter of wild conjecture, with vastly conflicting opinions as to the amounts consumed by the various guests, but in any event the festivities started in the main house with a pre-prandial drink or two, after which the group sauntered down to the elegant Oriental lake house where a home-style barbecue buffet was being served by Plummer Walker, an old Reynolds family retainer.*

According to Plummer Walker, after dinner, Libby and Mary Louise Vaught started "drinking corn whiskey shot for shot with home-brew chasers." Plummer said that Libby wanted to show Mrs. Vaught that she could "drink like a man," and during all this, Smith pouted. Plummer said later, upon questioning, "As you understand, I was here when he was a little boy. When he doesn't like things, I can tell by looking at him; he don't have to speak. I noticed down there that he didn't exactly like the way things were going." According to Machlin, the following events transpired later:

> *Around ten o'clock, Ab Walker, assuming somewhat the role of the host's alter ego, suggested that everybody who was finished canoeing or swimming come on up to the house for a drink afterwards, where they could listen to one of Libby's records on the Victrola.*
>
> *Between eleven and twelve, the guests sat around, had some drinks, chatted with one another, and departed.*

> *At about midnight, the watchman, making his rounds, saw Libby coming up through the bushes from the pool on the north side of the house. Walker met her outside. They exchanged a few words and walked into the house, where Smith met them at the door and took Libby upstairs.*

When Smith returned alone, he and Walker argued, and Walker left the bungalow to go outside. Smith went back upstairs. Later, Walker went back into the house, and suddenly he heard a voice calling to him from the east wing—Smith and Libby's bedroom. Before he got completely up the stairs, "Libby staggered out of the corridor, her lacy peach-colored negligee drenched with blood." She said, "Smith's killed himself" and then fainted. Walker found Smith "sprawled across the bed with a gaping wound in his temple."

Smith was taken to Baptist Hospital, where surgeons began to operate on him. Libby was given a private room on the third floor. Events took a turn for the worst:

> *At 5:25 A.M. the weary, blood-covered surgeons emerged from the operating room to announce that Reynolds was dead. Ab volunteered to bring the news to Libby, who was sleeping—or passed out—in Room 311, two floors below.*
>
> *The coroner, who arrived within an hour after the death was announced, pronounced the cause of death as suicide and declared that he could find "no motive" for Reynolds to have put himself to death.*
>
> *Newspapers speculated on other possible theories. The* Daily News *said: "Three questions remain to be answered and fully backed up by evidence. They are:*
>
> *Was 'Skipper'—as young Reynolds was known to a circuit of night clubs as well as a smart social set of Glen Cove, L.I.—murdered?*
>
> *Did the impetuous tobacco princeling kill himself because $20 million bored him?*
>
> *Did he shoot himself accidently while his torch-bearing bride from Broadway waited for him in their bedroom?*

According to various records, the coroner's inquest—"neither suicide nor murder"—led the case to a grand jury, sworn in on August 3, with all testimony being secret. The next day, the jury "issued a presentment charging that Libby Reynolds and Ab Walker, "on or about the sixth day of July, 1932, with force and arms, did unlawfully, willfully, feloniously, premeditatedly, of their malice aforethought murder Z. Smith Reynolds." It was a charge of first-degree murder punishable by death in the electric chair.

By five o'clock that evening, Ab Walker was in jail without bail. But Libby, ill and under the protection of her family—somewhere in Ohio, presumably—was nowhere to be found. Her father, when informed of the indictment, said, "My daughter's absolutely innocent. This is a frame-up and a terrible injustice to an innocent young woman."

Libby arrived in Wentworth, North Carolina, on August 9, "dashed from the train into a car with drawn blinds and later arrived at the courthouse in complete head-to-toe mourning, with a black veil hiding her face." She paid her $25,000 bond before she made "another spectacular dash into seclusion." By this time, Libby had announced her pregnancy to the world.

What happened next? According to Machlin, the Reynolds family "made its views public":

> *The words were couched very carefully. At one point, Will Reynolds' statement said simply that there was no "conclusive" proof of murder. There was no expression of sympathy or confidence in Libby. One paper reported, "It is known that the Reynolds tobacco dynasty is bringing powerful pressure…to drop the indictments on Wednesday to obviate the baring of Libby's and Smith's private lives before a jury." On November 15, Judge A.M. Stack announced that a* nolle prosequi *be entered in the records in the Libby Holman case. "Mr. Clark," the judge said, hammering his gavel, "let the defendants be discharged and their bonds be released." In the* Times, *the news of Libby's release was carried on the amusement page next to a review of a concert by Jascha Heifetz.*

Heidi Schnakenerg observes, "To this day, Smith's death is a mystery." She elaborates on several theories:

> *The most likely story is that Smith did threaten to commit suicide and held the gun to his head. Libby probably rushed across the room to stop him, and in the ensuing "scuffle," as Dick said, the revolver accidentally went off. Perhaps Smith's suicide threat was supposed to be a dramatic maneuver intended to manipulate Libby—but instead ended in tragedy. With his daring excursions and risky lifestyle, Smith had tempted death numerous times during his short life. But it was his emotional insecurities, not a stunt flight or mechanical failure over the Sahara, that ultimately led to his demise.*
>
> *No matter what happened, Libby refused to speak about the incident for the rest of her life. No one but Libby, and perhaps Ab, would ever know what really happened.*

An interesting postscript to the Smith-Libby saga is this: On January 11, 1933, Libby gave birth to a three-and-a-half-pound baby boy, Christopher Smith Reynolds, in Philadelphia. Libby and Christopher received one-fourth of Smith's estate, approximately $7 million. Smith's first wife, Anne Cannon, and baby Anne received 37 percent or $9 million, and Smith's siblings received the remainder. In addition, reports indicate that Libby got $750,000 from Dick as an incentive to cease litigation.

RAPE, POSSE, GUNFIRE

The following account is from the 1918 meeting notes of the City of Winston-Salem:

> *THE NOVEMBER 18 RIOT*
> *On Saturday, November 16, 1918, a white couple was strolling along the streets of north Winston when they were accosted by a black man who hit the man over the head with a pistol and dragged the woman down into a ravine and allegedly raped her. The sheriff was summoned to the scene and deputies began looking for a man fitting a somewhat vague description. They observed a man generally fitting the description and a pursuit began. The Sheriff joined in and the man turned and fired, hitting the Sheriff in the hand. The posse lost the assailant and the Sheriff ordered a roundup of suspects. A number of people were initially arrested. One man was taken to county jail where he was charged with rape.*
>
> *On Sunday afternoon, November 17, a large group of whites gathered on Courthouse Square and rumors of lynching began. By evening, the crowd had grown to 1,000. There was a lot of drinking and some of the crowd began to break into hardware stores and steal firearms to force a jailbreak. The Mayor and other civic leaders appeared and tried to reason with the crowd…to no avail.*
>
> *Eventually the Home Guard was called out (the Forsyth Riflemen having been activated for service in World War One and in Europe). The Home Guard was made of mostly old men and young boys; certainly not the disciplined paramilitary unit that made up the Forsyth Rifles. The Home Guard surrounded the jail and called for the fire department with the idea they could disperse the crowd using fire hoses. The hoses were aimed at the crowd and water turned on. Gunfire erupted from the direction of the crowd. Police, Sheriff's deputies and the home guard returned the fire.*

Rioters.

Several people were hit, including a 13 year old girl, killed by a stray bullet while watching from a second story window; a citizen who was part of the mob; a home guardsman; and Bob Young. Young had been a member of the Winston-Salem Police in 1903. Later, he was a city fireman. At the time of the riot, he was a shoe salesman. When the fire department was called to disperse the crowd, he helped man the hose…and died in the gunfire. Police Sgt. Cofer was wounded in the hand. Officer Robert Bryan was also injured and absent from duty for three weeks.

After this initial volley, the crowd broke and ran down 4th Street into the black residential section. Gunfire was heard throughout the night. Several black residents were killed for whom death certificates exist. Eyewitnesses say that many other blacks were killed as well, but their bodies were stuffed into culverts or thrown onto railroad boxcars and sent out of town.

The Mayor summoned National Guard troops from Charlotte and Greensboro. A tank was set up on the square. By daylight on Monday, while the night of gunfire and violence had ended, machine guns were set up

Soldiers on guard.

> *on Fourth Street aimed toward the black residential area in anticipation of a counterattack that never came.*
>
> *In the following days, a number of people were charged with inciting a riot and attempting to break into a public jail, which was then a capital offense. Sixteen white men were convicted and given sentences ranging from 6 to 14 months on the county road gang. One black man was convicted of the murder of a Southern Utilities Company worker and executed in Raleigh.*

THE DROP FELL AT 12:55—BROKE HIS NECK

The Thursday, February 8, 1894 issue of the *Sentinel* presented graphic details of Peter DeGraff's execution. "Peter DeGraff is dead!" is the first line of the article. Let's go back to the night of July 20, or the early morning hours of July 21, and historian Fambrough L. Brownlee's report:

> *Peter DeGraff killed Ellen Smith in a lonely piece of woods behind the Zinzendorf Hotel. It was, more or less, a lovers' spat, she having borne his*

> *illegitimate child. A night or so later, he returned to the scene of the crime, thus providing for his eventual undoing. On his last night among the living, he explained to a local reporter that someone had told him that if a murderer returns to the site of his misdeed and calls the name of the victim, the evil act would be undone. It was this Shakespearian touch that made the murder of Ellen Smith a local legend.*
>
> *DeGraff eluded the immediate hue and cry, and it was nearly a year later before he was arrested by Sheriff McArthur near Rural Hall. Tried and convicted, DeGraff was sentenced to be hanged on Thursday, February 8, 1894.*

The *Sentinel* article reveals that the crowd witnessing the hanging numbered at least six thousand—and perhaps even more. Wagons, carts and buggies crowded the road to the execution site out of town. Those who did not ride walked in a jovial, high-spirited manner, as if they were going to an entertaining social event rather than an execution.

At the chosen site, Sheriff McArthur read the death warrant, and then Peter DeGraff made a final speech, confessing to the murder and blaming "dice, cards, easy women, and hard liquor":

> *The devil had such a great power over me that I thought I could almost walk with death without fear. He said he would be with me.*
>
> *I again say don't put your hands on cards, bad women and dice. Hear my dying words. I have washed my blood and hope those who have enmity against me will forgive me.*
>
> *May God bless you all is my prayer on this side of the bar of God.*

After a prayer from Reverend H.A. Brown, DeGraff shook hands with his brothers, the preachers, the sheriff, Chief Bradford and Officer Adams. In addition, he presented his hat and Bible to his youngest brother. Sheriff McArthur "sprung the trigger" at 12:52 p.m., and DeGraff was dead. His neck was broken, so death happened at once. An interesting editorial comment made by the *Sentinel* reporter was this: "When the cap was removed after the prisoner was taken down, the features of the dead man were found to be perfectly natural."

According to Bob Waltz, the killing of Ellen Smith and the execution of Peter DeGraff have been the subject of several songs. One is sung to the tune of "How Firm a Foundation."

POOR ELLEN SMITH

Poor Ellen Smith, and it's how she was found,
Shot through the heart, lying cold on the ground.
Oh, I brushed back my tears when the people all said
That Peter DeGraff had shot Ellen Smith dead.

While I would have loved her and made her my wife,
Lord, I loved her too dearly to take her sweet life.
They grabbed their Winchesters, they hunted me down,
But I was away in old Mount Airy town.

They carried me to Winston, my trial to stand
To live or to die as the law may command.
McArthur will hang me, he will if he can;
God knows, if they hang me, I'll die an innocent man.

STATE PRISON ESCAPEE RECAPTURED AFTER TWENTY YEARS

The August 14, 1907 edition of the *Dispatch* ran an article about Calvin Westmoreland, an escaped convict, who was arrested in Winston-Salem after he had been at liberty for twenty years. Here is the true story of Westmoreland's odyssey:

> *He was sentenced from Danbury, Stokes County, February 2, 1887, for larceny and served two years of his three-year sentence. In 1887, while the convicts were working on the old Cape Fear & Yadkin Valley railroad, Westmoreland escaped Jan. 17, 1887.*

Where was Westmoreland and what was he doing during those twenty years? According to the newspaper article, he had been living in Winston-Salem for the last ten years of his freedom. He married and had children; he worked as a carpenter. How was he discovered? The Winston-Salem jailor received notice from penitentiary officials offering a ten-dollar reward for his arrest and delivery. Apparently, the jailor did his homework because it was only a matter of days before he discovered Westmoreland's whereabouts and arrested him in the Farmers' Warehouse.

Although he denied all charges and even the fact that he had ever been incarcerated, Westmoreland's wife told the jailor, "Why, he served over half his sentence before he escaped." Upon further examination, Westmoreland admitted to his escape, living in Stokes County the first ten years and then moving on to Winston-Salem for the last ten. His comment upon capture was this: "They say I have one year and fifteen days of my sentence yet to serve."

What was the original larceny? Westmoreland was found guilty of stealing a secondhand still.

Acquaintances knew all along that Westmoreland was living as an escaped convict in Winston-Salem, but they, too, felt that he had served enough time for stealing an old still.

Mob Storms Jail

Note: The events of November 16 and 17, 1918, were recorded in practically every newspaper in the state of North Carolina. Included here are two rather obscure records of the infamous riot—one from the minutes of the City of Winston-Salem Direction Board (1913–19) and one from the New York Times.

The November 18, 1918 edition of the *New York Times* had four bold captions: "Southern Raceriot [*sic*] Costs Five Lives—Army Tank Corps Called to Quell a Lynching Mob in Winston-Salem, N.C.—Battle with Home Guards—Jail-Storming Crowd Overcomes Them, as Well as Police and Fire Companies." According to the article, the riot came about as a mob stormed the jail and lynched a Negro prisoner. At least five people were killed and others injured. Among the dead were Rachael Levi, a bystander, and Robert Young, a fireman. Following are specifics concerning the mob storming the jail:

> *The mob first formed this afternoon about 3:30 o'clock, and stormed the jail. Three shots were fired, and the negro accused of shooting the two men and attacking Mrs. Childress was seriously wounded, while a white prisoner named Tragg also was hit in the arm by a stray bullet.*
>
> *After some difficulty the police succeeded in clearing the crowd out of the building, and then the Mayor called out the Home Guards. Quiet reigned for a time, but later the report went around that the Negro shot was not the man that had been sought. By nightfall the mob had reformed and started marching to the jail, which was surrounded by Home Guards.*

Join the Tank Corps.

Governor Bickett sent 250 members of a tank battalion to help quell the riot, and the Greensboro Home Guards went by special train to the Twin Cities to assist. The mob had broken into hardware stores and stolen revolvers, shotguns and ammunition, and as the mob increased in size—reportedly, to as many as several thousand—the men marched toward the jail. Although the mayor attempted to calm the crowd, he could not be heard over the noise, so fireman, who had arrived at the scene, turned their water hoses on the men. This did not deter them, and they began firing. The Home Guards returned fire; however, the mob overpowered them. They entered the jail. A couple of guards, who were guarding the inside, were badly injured by members of the mob throwing them down a stairwell.

When the mob did not find the African American it was looking for, it ceased fire, left the jail and marched through the business section of Winston-Salem. Some of the men headed toward the "Negro quarter" of town. The newspaper article ends with the sentence: "Late tonight, however, there had been no clash between the whites and blacks."

According to one historian, "The number of causalities will never be known. Death certificates were filed for five white men and one black, George Johnson, a twenty-two-year-old machinery hand at R.J. Reynolds Tobacco Company." Other details follow:

> *Eyewitnesses, including one man on duty at the jail that night, state that bodies of a number of blacks were stuffed into railroad culverts or thrown into Belo's Pond. Estimates of the number of blacks killed range as high as fifty, although a somewhat lower number is more likely.*
>
> *Fifteen white men received sentences of from fourteen months to six years on the county roads. One black man, Will Davis, was executed for the murder of a Southern Public Utilities Company worker. The original target of the mob was found not guilty of rape on the testimony of the victim.*

Part III

Now You Know

He Claimed He Could Heal Anything—For a Price

The front-page caption read, "Winston-Salem Negro Is Held on Fraud Charge." The date was September 15, 1950. The story focused on forty-year-old Johnnie B. Barnes, alias Professor B.B. Barnes. The complaint concerned post office inspector R.S. Fisher accusing Barnes of fraud by mail. A federal warrant was then issued by Charles E. Ader, U.S. commissioner, on complaints made from South Boston and Roanoke, Virginia. This is how authorities caught Barnes:

> *Barnes' big mistake, however, was in attempting to deal with Post Office Inspector Fisher, who took the name of Lucy Wells, a Negro woman, and asked if Barnes would cure her backache for $10. According to the federal report of investigation, Barnes sent Lucy Wells—or Fisher—150 tablets, which a local doctor told the post office inspector wouldn't do him any harm—or any good, either.*

Barnes was subsequently arrested by a U.S. marshal and given a federal hearing. No newspaper account has appeared in print announcing the outcome of that hearing.

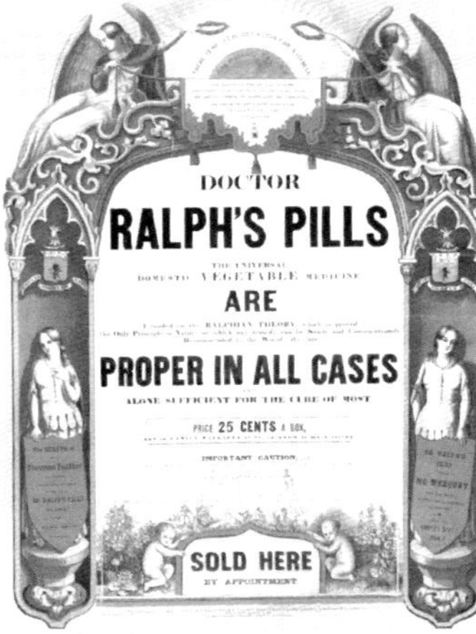

Left: Cathartic pills.

Above: Doctor Ralph's pills.

Below: Inhaling tube, catarrh cure and mandrake and horehound pills.

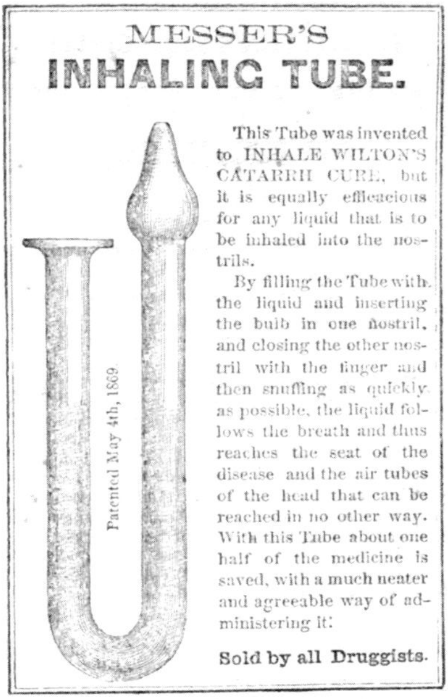

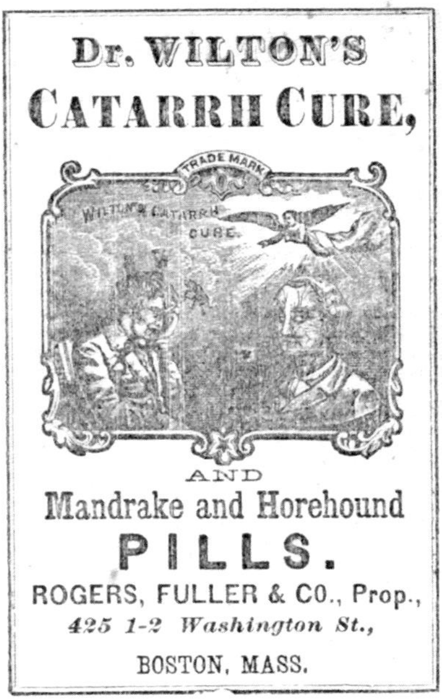

Not in My Neighborhood

It seems that the location of Winston-Salem's first garbage incinerator met with some pretty wicked opposition for a couple of years, as noted in the minutes of the Directing Board. The idea of purchasing an incinerator came up at the May 26, 1914 meeting, but no action was taken "until the Mayor could go to Raleigh and examine the one there."

At the June 2, 1914 meeting, the mayor said he had visited Raleigh "but found that the incinerator was not as great as he expected. The plant would only consume from fifteen to eighteen one-horse loads of paper per day."

At their August 7, 1914 board meeting, the group voted to empower the Sanitary Committee to find a place for the garbage incinerator. There was no further mention until March 16, 1915, when the Sanitary Committee suggested North Trade Street near Eighth as a suitable place; however, "a group of property owners protested." The next day, the committee suggested the west side of Chestnut between Fifth and Sixth; however, property owners in that area also "protested the installation of the incinerator at that location." Finally, the board suggested a location on "the north side of Peters Creek just west of Underwood Avenue, being part of the old water works property in the Belo's Pond area." The final entry in the minutes contained this sentence: "On April 6, 1915, Mayor Eaton reported that the incinerator had been completed and was working fine."

Lust for Fashionable Apparel

Old Salem: The Official Guidebook includes a section entitled "Testing the Rules." After the Revolutionary War, the board governing the Moravian congregations warned that "too many people were beginning to feel the spirit of the freedom in the land." The board's concern was that members of the Moravian congregation would "lose control of their children and forget their daily devotions." In addition, some people had begun neglecting attendance at the Singstunden." They also changed their views "about the church, about race, about dress, and about ways of doing business with each other and with the outside world." That was not all. By 1800, Moravians began to challenge the practice of using the "Lot" to make decisions, especially about marriages. By 1787, the church boards addressed the problem of the "new fashions which are slipping in among us" and the "lust for fashionable apparel."

Such things are, such things were.

Elders expressed their displeasure with this new trend in no uncertain terms:

> *In the first place it should be noted that a desire for fashionable dress is at bottom a wish to wear something different, something new, and so become noticeable and attract attention. Among such things are the big, shaggy hats; the hats with dropping brims, down which hang cords, or a pretty ribbon or an unusual buckle. Colors also come under the head when they are chosen to*

> *strike the eye, or when they are variegated; or when Clothing is adorned with silver or gilt or other shining buttons, and when coat and vest and breeches each has a conspicuous color.*

Consequently, all were admonished to "dress according to their station, and a poor person should not have the clothes which one more well-to-do might properly purchase."

The Dreaded Invaders Arrived

In her article entitled "Glimpses of Small-Town Winston," Mary C. Wiley writes about the only time Winston was invaded by enemy troops during the Civil War. The date was April 10, 1965, and approximately three thousand cavalrymen "passed through the town and encamped for the night beyond Salem Creek." What happened before their arrival is a true story of the quick thinking of clerk of court John Blackburn to protect valuable records:

> *The men on the lookout for the enemy came dashing back from Liberty to the Square with word that the dreaded invaders had actually appeared on the outskirts of the town.*

Cavalry marching.

In his graphic way, Clerk of Court Blackburn makes us see his nervous haste as, searching through his records in the unguarded courthouse, he tumbles the most valuable of the papers into a sack, and with sack over his shoulders, journals and minute books under his arm, rushes out of the building across the street to the Widow Long's house to deposit with her the sack, and then on to Mrs. Emily Webb's and to Franklin L. Gorrell's with his other documents.

After Blackburn had delivered all the important documents to Widow Long, Mrs. Webb and Mr. Gorrell, he felt better, knowing that the Northern soldiers would never look in these secret hiding places. He then met up with Salem folks, waving white handkerchiefs as symbols of surrender. "One of our company," writes Blackburn, "introduced himself to General Palmer and then introduced the others to him, and he introduced us to several of his officers and invited us to accompany him into town. Which we did."

ALDERMAN "BLASTED" MAYOR

The February 13, 1945 minutes of the Winston-Salem Directing Board began with this sentence, "Alderman Stockton blasted Mayor Coan for issuing a statement to the newspaper proposing The Coan Plan for forgiving taxes of the men and women in the armed forces." This forgiving policy, according to the minutes, would result in $34,000 to $68,000 in lost taxes each year for three years. Stockton called the plan "political" and added, "It does appear that in a matter of this kind when so much money is involved that the Mayor would take the matter up with the Finance Committee or the Board of Aldermen."

The minutes of the meeting also include the Board versus Coan controversy in a rather uncomplimentary way:

For almost two years members of this Board have talked with Mayor Coan and tried to get him to take up such matters with this Board before breaking out in the newspapers with them. The Mayor's position has been that since he was elected by all the people he was elected to run the city government and the Aldermen should bow to his will. Our City Charter set up no such one-man government, and until it is changed to do so I feel that we should operate under the Aldermanic System as set up.

When Mayor Coan took office he stated that one of the reasons he ran for Mayor was to get his name on the front page of the newspapers. If the

> *Mayor has to use such methods as the Coan Plan to keep his name on the front page I believe it would be advisable to miss one issue.*
>
> *Stockton then blasted the Mayor for the confusion that exists on site selection for the new hospital and discussed the two proposed sites—one at 4th and Broad and the other, the so-called 30-acre site in the area of Miller Street south of West First.*

So how did Mayor Coan respond? He said he didn't feel like talking and would give an answer to every statement at the next meeting but went on to refute some of Alderman Stockton's charges. At the next board meeting, Coan distributed two issues of the local newspaper—where he had, ironically, responded in print.

"Other Such Business"

A special meeting of the Directing Board was called on June 29, 1951. The routine business session considered several prospective ordinances; however, the "other such business" made this "one of the most memorable meetings in City Government." This is what transpired, according to the recorded minutes:

> *Mayor Kurfees stated, "At this time we have been requested to have a hearing by Mrs. Collins who was a pharmacist at the City Memorial Hospital and has been discharged. So at this time and without further ado, I will appreciate it, Mrs. Collins, if you will come around. Mrs. Collins, I believe you called and requested that you have a hearing before the Board of Aldermen and I stated to you that I felt that the proper place to have this hearing was maybe before the Hospital Commission. You stated to me that due to the fact that the Administrator, and the City Manager, and also one of the doctors more or less involved were on the Hospital Commission that you would appreciate a hearing before this Body. So, as this is Democracy in action, we will be glad to hear from you at this time.*

Let's review what preceded Mrs. Collins's appearing before the board of aldermen. Collins, who had been fired as chief pharmacist at the hospital, said her dismissal was the result of a "personality conflict." City manager C.E. Perkins, who backed his department head, said that her professional ability was not part of the controversy and that she had considerable support. The board of aldermen went into a discussion of the matter, with subsequent minutes covering eighteen pages. Mayor Kurfees is reported as issuing the following statement:

> *As long as I am Mayor of the City of Winston-Salem everybody is going to have a fair hearing. After proper consideration if the Board of Aldermen desire to make recommendations to the City Manager, well and good; if it doesn't desire to make any recommendations to him, that, too, is well and good. I realize that department heads have a perfect right to hire and fire in their discretion. I think that it is up to the Board of Aldermen and the City Manager whether or not the proper discretion has been used in this case. So without further ado on that, does any member of the Board have anything he would like to bring up at this time?*

The minutes indicate the next action: "Then the bomb dropped." Alderman Tucker spoke: "I would like to make a motion, Mr. Mayor. I move that Mr. C.E. Perkins be discharged as City Manager effective as now, and I further move that the City Treasurer be authorized to execute and deliver a check to him for one month's pay." Alderman Chitty seconded the motion. Next, Alderman Fulp asked the city attorney if that would be offered in the form of a motion. The following discussion about the legality of a motion went back and forth.

Mr. Carlyle, city attorney, informed the group—in a long and often repetitive speech—that the city manager could only be removed by a resolution adopted by two-thirds of the board, the purpose of which was to prevent hasty action. He went on to inform everyone that Mr. Tucker's motion could not be considered a resolution—mainly because it was not in writing.

Alderman Fulp made a lengthy speech praising the capabilities of Mr. Perkins and then turned his attention to Alderman Tucker, speaking about him in a frank manner:

> *I am a little bit shocked; I am amazed as a matter of fact, that any such thing could be done. I would like to offer my advice to the man that offered this motion; that he take counsel with himself and speak with somebody with an open mind. I think that perhaps he has spoken to a lot of people that might have a little grudge. I am not making that as an absolute statement, but I am saying that might be so. I think we are doing a very dangerous thing.*

Mayor Kurfees spoke next, thanking the city attorney for his legal knowledge in the matter, and then made his final statements:

> *The Board of Aldermen of the City of Winston-Salem was elected by the people of Winston-Salem by a majority vote. Under the law adopted at Raleigh establishing the City Manager form of government it specifically states that the City Manager shall be employed at the pleasure of the Board of Alderman. I am very reluctant to go against the advice of our City Attorney…and he usually knows what he is talking about, but not withstanding that fact, gentlemen, I will have to adhere to this motion.*

The minutes of this meeting consist of twenty-six pages. The motion to discharge the city manager passed five to two.

An interesting aside concerns a book of fiction entitled *The Checker Board Corridor* by Rixie Hunter. The book "details the conflict between Perkins and Kurfees with the names changed."

Racially Tense Winston-Salem

A November 4, 1967 newspaper article entitled "Weird Friday Night" explored the following aftermath of a race riot in the city:

> *Friday night in North Carolina's second largest city is usually a busy one. Stores normally stay open until 9 p.m., and the streets are filled with people engaging in social activities or just window-shopping.*
>
> *Downtown Winston-Salem was bare on this Friday night except for a few cars. Stores were closed. Few people were in sight. Only the occasional scream of a siren pierced the unreal silence. Fresh sheets of plywood covered store windows.*
>
> *Armed policemen at Third and Church Streets crunched broken glass under their boots as they hoped for a quiet night, instead of a recurrence of Thursday's racial violence. National Guardsmen in freshly-starched fatigues stood at every corner with fixed bayonets. They appeared very young and uncertain of what was really happening.*
>
> *An old car, its muffler making a little too much noise, entered the block. Suddenly a police car appeared behind it, its blue light outflashing the few lighted neon signs. Another approached it from the front, and still another came out of Church Street.*

Within seconds, 20 police officers surrounded the car with drawn pistols and sawed-off riot shotguns. "Get out with your hands up," one of the officers shouted.

Police leaned the youths against the car in spread-eagle position, balanced precariously so they could easily be tripped if they moved while they were frisked. Other officers searched the trunk and interior of the car for weapons. A few moments later the youths were allowed to go.

On Liberty Street two blocks away, paper stickers remained on several plate-glass windows which had just been placed in store fronts. The area had been heavily hit Thursday night, but no shattered glass or trash was on the street. Merchants had spent the sunny day cleaning up.

So, what events had taken place the night before? According to one newspaper report, the violence on Thursday night was called "the worst racial outbreak in the century in North Carolina" and came about after the funeral of "a Negro man clubbed to death by a white policeman who said the man was drunk and disorderly." Approximately five hundred Negros rioted, according to one report. Sniper fire broke out on Thursday night about 10:30 p.m. at Fourteenth and Liberty Streets. Fires, started by Molotov cocktails, "flared in the downtown area and fire damage was estimated at more than $500,000."

On Friday night, rock throwing, looting and arson were reported. In addition, snipers "fired a shot that passed through the clothing of a guardsman. He was not hurt."

One newspaper article reported arrests:

Police said 105 persons had been arrested since Thursday night and 45 persons, including eight policemen, injured. Twenty-two fires were set Friday night as gangs staged hit-and-run arson attacks on stores.

Police at one point fired over the heads of a group of Negroes before sealing off a 10 block section of the downtown area. Officers later reported that snipers were taking "pot shots" at them in the Negro district.

Police later rushed a house from where they said shots were being fired and arrested nine persons.

AT THE ZINZENDORF HOTEL

On Thanksgiving Day 1892, the recently opened Zinzendorf Hotel—with room rates at three dollars a day—was destroyed by fire that broke out in the laundry room. Both Winston and Salem firemen answered the alarm. Andrew J. Peddycord of Salem's Rough and Ready Fire Company drove the Salem fire engine to the burning hotel and saw W.F. Keith, the Winston steam engineer, headed to the Zinzendorf. Keith's vehicle, according to historical reports, "was not propelled by its own steam but hitched to the back of a streetcar, with engineer Keith seated on the top of the car." Then the following incidents unfolded:

> *"I'll go by 'em this time!" declared the veteran fireman, and dropping the driving reins on his fine pair of black horses, he holloed* [sic], *"Go!" and gave chase to the streetcar.*
>
> *When he reached the old Walker tobacco factory, he shouted "Good-bye!" to the Winston firemen and dashed by their streetcar-driven steamer.*
>
> *When, however, the gallant drive of old Rough and Ready reached the hotel, laid out the hose line and coupled it to the hydrant, he found there was no water.*
>
> *All the heroic firemen of both towns could do was to load their hose and watch the fire destroy the most magnificent hotel Winston had ever erected. The fire was so intense that the heat was felt blocks away and the Davis School cadets and volunteer firemen were kept busy putting out fires on the roofs of adjacent buildings caught by sparks from the flying shingles of the burning hotel.*

Hotel guests had earlier carried out their belongings and some of the hotel furniture as "the whole town sat back to watch. It was the event of the year."

Ironic is the fact that on this Thanksgiving Day 1892, the Hotel Zinzendorf's chefs rose early to prepare a splendid feast. R.J. Reynolds and several other hunters went into the woods and shot wild turkeys and quail to complement delicious side dishes made by the staff. According to one historical report, this is what happened:

> *By 11:00 a.m. the aromas of fresh-baked bread and roasted turkey with all the trimmings filled the halls. Hotel guests gathered outside the dining room, expecting someone to announce, "Dinner is served." Instead they heard a shout from the laundry room: Fire! Fire! Flames shot from the rear of the grand hotel. People grabbed furniture, fixtures, and personal possessions as they ran out the doors. Cadets from Davis School plunged into the burning building to rescue guests and property. With its wooden frame and cedar shingles, the Hotel Zinzendorf stood no chance against the hungry fire.*

Fortunately, nobody was seriously hurt. An impromptu Thanksgiving Day "picnic on the grounds" was quickly organized; however, this feast lacked the turkey and quail bagged by Reynolds and his hunter friends.

MORAVIANS IN SALEM "GOING AGAINST TRADITION"

Throughout their book *Old Salem: The Official Guidebook*, authors Penelope Niven and Cornelia Wright reveal the ways in which Moravians in Salem digressed from strict rules and regulations. Some of the congregation's younger men and women began desiring clothing that was fancier than the recommended garb. In 1787, elders "expressed their displeasure with this new trend in no uncertain terms."

In 1799, married Brother Thomas Butner was chosen to be the baker for this Moravian community. Things did not go well because Brother Butner was discovered "selling hard cider to the youths of the town." Christian Winkler bought the bakery in 1808. Although most of Brother Winkler's sons worked diligently at the Winkler Bakery, built in 1800, Henry Winkler was called a "rebel" because of his "too liberal use of spirituous liquor."

In 1790, Dr. Samuel Benjamin Vierling arrived in Salem, and "with little if any anesthesia for his patients, he pulled teeth, amputated gangrenous limbs, removed cataracts, operated for cancer of other maladies, and even performed brain surgery." When he reviewed the high number of strokes among Salem residents, he connected that medical problem with the salt-treated pork that families were consuming. Consequently, the Market-Fire House was established in 1803 to provide fresh meat.

In *The Three Forks of Muddy Creek*, editor Frances Griffin paints a good picture of the Salem Tavern:

> *For it was here that men of all factions and dispositions gathered over tankards of ale and tumblers of good peach brandy, sometimes only to argue and talk and other times to duel with fists and pistols, gouging out eyes and biting off each others lips—or if they were of the officer class, seeking requisitions in beef and lead and beer, all of which was paid for (if paid for at all) in worthless wartime currency or in "tickets" to be held against the prospect of peace and redemption by an independent state legislature.*

Griffin reveals the Moravian rules regarding the tavern keeper. He must not allow guests to take drinks to their rooms. He could not engage in playing

Salem Tavern, Winston-Salem, North Carolina.

cards or other gaming. He must watch for wrongdoers, but above all, "he must not allow Salem residents to feast and drink in the tavern":

> *He may allow members of the Congregation, who own businesses in the place, to take a stranger into the tavern, and treat him according to the circumstances, with food and drink, but he must not allow a company of inhabitants of the place to set themselves together as guests, in order to drink and feast, which is seriously prohibited, and the Host if permitted, and even commanded, to admonish and speak seriously to such inhabitants of Salem who come together*

> *for gossip, or loafing, or unnecessary acquaintance with strangers, or curiosity, when found around or inside the tavern, and to remind them to go to their business, or if it be Sunday, to go to their respective dwelling houses.*

So, the tavern keeper's job was extremely difficult. By 1775, when a report spread throughout Salem that it had become a habit of the single brothers to frequent the tavern, where "they had a gay time," the tavern keeper was informed that part of his duty was "to send those people away" because "the tavern is for travelling strangers only."

A decision was made to establish a liquor shop in the Single Brothers House, a place "where the Brothers...can buy, now and then, a limited amount of brandy which has been distilled in their own distillery." According to historians, those travelers were "crusty, hard-drinking veterans of wars, adventurers like Daniel Boone, evangelists, peddlers and blackguards."

Brother Jacob Meyer would always remember the date—June 22, 1776—when he almost lost his life:

> *Four drunken militiamen, armed with clubs, guns and tomahawks, wantonly attacked Brother and Sister Meyer, and later when these same strangers*

Daniel Boone fighting.

> *forced their way into the Single Brothers House, again laying about them with tomahawks and guns, leaving five of the residents critically wounded and the house itself a shambles before being subdued and brought to trial. Assessed a fine then carted off to Salisbury where they were supposed to begin serving a jail sentence but where, instead, they were immediately set free, presumably by a judge who shared much of the backcountry's contempt for the Moravians and their alleged policy of neutrality.*

The Salem tavern keeper definitely had to multitask, as we understand that term today. He had to be supplier, server and bouncer.

As if that were not enough for poor Brother Jacob Meyer and the entire population of Salem, wickedness had not finished its task, as illustrated here:

> *Even more terrible times were ahead for Brother Meyer and for the entire town as the British and American armies moved north from Cowpens and Kings Mountain, on their way to the bloody and pivotal battle at Guilford Courthouse. American militiamen, freebooters, regular army men—all descended upon the town in force, pillaging at will and often attempting to force the Moravians into admitting a collusion with the British, hauling away countless stores for which the congregation was never paid and threatening the Brethren, individually and collectively, with imminent disaster.*

After the air had cleared from the looting and pillaging, Jacob Meyer's life took another turn for the worse. Salem Tavern caught on fire early one morning. Meyer and his wife awoke to find their bedroom filled with smoke; a couple of male lodgers helped get them outside. They were safe; however, Meyer kept fretting over an earlier feeling that he had been duly warned of the fire. This is what he reported to the elders:

> *He had been overcome by a feeling of trouble without knowing why; that he had prayed to the Lord for new grace and forgiveness and had felt that all was well. Yet this was not enough, and he had been brought to consider how much grace and mercy the Saviour had showed to him, and that he could not think of one room or one little place in the house where the Saviour had not showed him special graces. In spite of the blessing which accompanied this experience he had felt the trouble constantly until he went to sleep last night. And in spite of the terrible sequel he could not thank the Lord enough that He had held His hand over him and his family; for in a quarter of an hour the flames would have overcome them.*

Salem workmen eventually rebuilt the tavern, and Meyer and his wife were back as tavern keepers. All was still not well because eventually the congregation became extremely unhappy with the drinking habits of their young men. Stagecoach drivers and card players at the tavern apparently "attracted youth and had a bad influence on them." Meyer and his wife retired, but according to various reports, "Meyer lived for thirteen years after leaving the tavern, but retirement did not always agree with him, particularly after his health had forced him to cease all physical activity. Idleness bred in him a kind of self-inflicted torture."

ANYTHING WICKED "GOES" FOR A NEWS SNIPPET

At the very earliest part of the twentieth century, newspapers printed "glimpses" of wickedness without giving the entire story. Perhaps the following snippets appear in print to whet readers' appetites to learn more. Perhaps that's all the reporter could "dig up:"

> *Eleven-year-old John Diggs, while swinging from a train at Winston-Salem, fell and got his foot mashed under a wheel. He was doing what so many youngsters do—riding a train out of the railway yards. (November 8, 1905)*
>
> *Mr. Paul C. Lindley, of Pomona, has instituted suit against the Fries Power and Manufacturing Company, of Winston-Salem, on account of injuries received by him in being thrown from his automobile, which was struck by a street car, in the suburbs of Winston-Salem several weeks ago...His hip was badly hurt in the accident and he is not yet able to get around without the aid of crutches. (November 8, 1905)*
>
> *H.A. Lineback, a photographer of Winston, has been informed that two fakirs have traveled Davie county representing themselves to be his agents, taking pictures of farm houses and collecting for them, saying the Winston photographer will send the pictures as soon as they are finished up. He has no agents and the two fakirs are out on their own book. (August 15, 1906)*
>
> *The Winston-Salem tobacco men are kicking against the improper handling of shipments of leaf tobacco by the railroads. They have appealed to the corporation commission for relief. (October 24, 1906)*

Old farmhouse.

John Brandon, who lives two miles from Winston, lost a cow last week by lightning. He was 20 feet from the animal, which was chained to a stake when the bolt came. It was not raining then. Seeing the cow down, feebly kicking, he ran to her, loosed the chain and patted her on the side, saying, "Poor Daisy," and he didn't remember much after that. The cow was a battery full of electric power, or else a second bolt came, for Brandon was knocked silly, and his hair and eyebrows burned. (January 17, 1908)

Fifteen years ago a Winston-Salem plug tobacco factory put in new machinery and men were sent from a northern firm to do the work. One of them left with a box of tobacco from the plant. The other day he sent $4, saying he had reformed. The money was sent back to him to use in spreading the Word. Dr.

Lightning.

David F. Houseton, born in North Carolina 42 years ago, is now chancellor of Washington University. (June 17, 1908)

Yesterday morning about 10 o'clock six men were killed and one badly injured near Winston-Salem in a land-slide, on the Southbound. The men were working in the Salem creed valley where a 600-foot railroad bridge is being constructed.

Above: David F. Houseton.

Below: Landslide.

> *They were 50 feet from the top of the hill where excavation was going on, when the tons of earth came down upon them. Some managed to escape from the slide, but six were simply smothered to death. (November 17, 1909)*
>
> *J.H. Eaton, a colored druggist of Winston-Salem, was fined $300 and costs in the recorder's court of that city Monday for selling liquor. (August 31, 1910)*

Sometimes, these snippets are more interesting than more detailed reporting. Probably intended years and years ago as simply "fillers," they certainly attract the reader's attention.

HE SAID, SHE SAID

R.J. Reynolds Jr. (Dick) and his wife, Blitz Dillard Reynolds, were divorced in 1946, and Blitz was awarded $9 million in cash and assets for their four sons. She also received the town house, Merry Acres, and the couple's country estate, Devotion. Author Heidi Schnakenberg calls this "the most lucrative divorce settlement in U.S. history," but it was fraught with maneuvers. These maneuvers were intended "to knock [Dick's] unsuspecting opponent [Blitz] off balance." Dick's actions are explained by Schnakenberg:

> *On September 21, 1945, at 6:30 A.M., Dick finally called Blitz and said he was in New York, stopping for a visit. What Dick was really doing was seeking the advice of lawyers in New York and courting Marianne. When Blitz asked him what he was doing there and when he would be back home, he hung up. Blitz was baffled by the call, and she didn't hear from him for another five days.*

At this time, Dick asked Blitz for a divorce; he wanted to marry his new lover. Blitz received a letter from Dick expressing his love for her and their four boys and also pouring his heart out that he could not wait to see them. This has been recorded as a "smoke-screen play to catch her off guard as he initiated divorce proceedings." Nevertheless, Blitz did not know this at the time, so she begged Dick to return home. Dick refused and told her not to even think about fighting the divorce or he would report her actions to Walter Winchell, "leaving Blitz embarrassed and ashamed." Historical reports indicate that Dick had already told Winchell about his upcoming divorce, and the news had already been announced on his radio show.

Dick decided to travel to Winston-Salem, and Blitz mistakenly thought her husband intended to reconcile, but that was not the case. Dick went to Winston-Salem to see his boys and gather his belongings. When Blitz realized this was her husband's intent, she refused to allow him into Merry Acres. Retaliation followed:

> *Dick phoned all the stores where he kept credit accounts for her and the kids and had them closed. Dick then left town. In November, he called Blitz at five o'clock in morning and simply said, "You will never know how much I hate you." Blitz had had enough. When Dick filed for divorce, he argued that he had told his wife he had no intention of living with her...and accused her of "mental cruelty" and an "ungovernable temper." Blitz countersued. She then filed for divorce in Forysth County. She accused Dick of "extreme" cruelty and said he publically embarrassed her, verbally abused her, and deserted her and their sons. She said it would be detrimental to the children to be around their father and that she should be awarded full custody.*

The divorce was finalized in 1946, and according to records, Blitz was awarded $9 million in cash and assets for their sons, along with the town house, Merry Acres, and their country estate, Devotion. Dick's boys would not see him for another two years. As for Dick, he married his second wife, Marianne, on August 7, 1946, and for a while they enjoyed a short-lived, extravagant lifestyle.

When Marianne became pregnant with their second child, Dick became "enraged" and said this was her way of getting more of his money. Dick drank more. Marianne began smoking during her pregnancy, and they spent more and more time apart. In addition, Marianne accused Dick of faking illnesses, kicked him out of the bedroom and inquired of the servants, "What happened to the dope?" or "Where is the body."

After Dick's sixth son, Patrick, was born in December 1948, Dick and Marianne vowed to sober up, but this lifestyle of sobriety quickly changed to one of drinking parties, which resulted in verbal and physical abuse:

> *Dick often became furious when Marianne wore revealing clothing in the presence of other men, which was the primary source of their arguments. Once Dick tackled Marianne to the ground in a choke hold and she pushed him back against a fireplace mantel, knocking him unconscious. When the fights were really bad, she hurled furniture and dishes at him and mocked him for being a coward when he didn't fight back. On one occasion,*

> *Marianne backed Dick up against the wall of their garage, cursed at him, and said, "You're a sissy, why don't you stand up and fight?" Then she picked up objects in the garage and threw them at him. Most of them broke on the floor, but one hit him and cut his forehead…In record time, the romance and the marriage had spiraled into violence and loathing.*

Enter Muriel Marston Greenough, socialite and former British correspondent for the *New York Times.* Dick met Muriel at a Waldorf-Astoria charity ball. Later, they went to Dick's apartment, drank martinis and talked. Muriel learned that Dick Reynolds came from one of the richest tobacco families in the country. In May 1951, Muriel and Dick ran into each other at the Ritz, and during lunch, Dick confessed to Muriel that he and his wife had not been getting along; he said they fought, and she would disappear to be with notorious playboy Porfirio Rubirosa. It wasn't until the affair with Rubirosa became public that Dick knew the marriage was over.

Intimate dinners followed. Those meals included a great deal of liquor. One night, Dick passed out at Muriel's home. Having been miserable in his marriage, Dick decided to end his marriage with Marianne; however, his second wife, who had two small boys, had other ideas. Dick's offer of a generous divorce settlement did not change her mind. Marianne remained uncooperative during the conversations the two had from time to time. After Marianne stole Dick's wallet, passport and clothes during one of his drunken episodes when he was passed out, he vowed never to go anywhere near her again. He was afraid that any subsequent meeting would end in his being "taken care of." Dick and Marianne were divorced on August 7, 1952.

The very next day, Dick and Muriel were married—but not before Dick presented Muriel with a prenuptial agreement, which limited the amount of money Muriel could take from him if they ever got divorced and "waived Muriel's right to anything more from Dick than the trusts he had already set up and about $100,000 worth of jewelry that he had already given her. Dick also presented her with a gift of $10,000."

Muriel returned the surprise. She said she would go along with the prenuptial if Dick would agree to something: stop drinking hard liquor. If he signed that agreement and then broke it, he would owe her $15,000 and his prenup would be null and void. According to one historian, "They both signed."

Dick and Muriel's marriage saw Dick's continued bad health—drinking and heavy smoking—during the mid-1950s. Although it was quite obvious that Dick was not meeting the terms of Muriel's prenuptial, she continued to try to get him to stop drinking, and it is written that Muriel took out her anger toward Dick on the servants.

Muriel was pregnant, so she rested while Dick adjourned to the bar. The Reynoldses' pregnancy ended when Muriel was mugged on a New York City street and miscarried. Life went on. In 1956, they returned to Winston-Salem to attend the dedication ceremony for Wake Forest's new campus. Then, in 1957, doctors discovered that Dick had a "low, nearly inactive sperm count, and their hopes for a child were gone." He continued to drink. At one point, Muriel announced to guests that her husband would not be joining them. "He'd be better off dead," she said. And, many times, Dick did "accuse Muriel of trying to kill him." Maybe he thought he had something to worry about because "Muriel carried a six-inch knife around with her at all times." The couple had been married for seven years when "Dick's drinking and mood swings [became] more than Muriel could bear, and Dick, who was very down-to-earth in spite of his wealth, grew to loathe Muriel's high-handed snobbery."

On August 16, 1959, Dick's lawyer, Frank Well, handed Muriel divorce papers. The grounds were "mental cruelty." Dick, wheezing into his oxygen mask, took the stand and gave the following testimony:

> *As he sat in the box, he again accused Muriel of vicious cruelty and of trying to kill him. He brought up the time Muriel had allegedly ordered the servants to salt his food and said she blew smoke in his face when he was trying to quit smoking...Dick then claimed Muriel was really trying to kill him with cruelty. He said that Muriel got him so upset that he threw up his lunches. "Two months prior to her leaving, I had lunch brought in on a tray, and she'd say, "This food is slop, it's trash, the cook is no good, you ought to throw it all in the garbage can." I'd say, "Please leave this room. Let me eat in peace for god's sake." And she wouldn't leave.*
>
> *Then Dick accused Muriel of forcing him to sell his 25,000 shares of RJR Tobacco stock too early. Dick expressed resentment over Muriel having a "whopping good time" with her mother. Then Dick charged Muriel with the oldest claim yet—he said Muriel had faked her pregnancy to stop him from divorcing her in 1954...Dick said there was never any proof that she was pregnant or miscarried and it was evidence of her deceiving ways. Dick's claims were never proven, and Muriel produced all of the doctor's reports and the certificate of fetal death in response.*

During the divorce hearing between Dick and Muriel, Dr. Annemarie Schmitt Reynolds entered the picture. Muriel's lawyers accused Dick of adultery and bigamy. Muriel was able to produce for the court a marriage certificate and a statement by Reverend Charles Nabers, who had married them. Annemarie had refused a subpoena delivered to her on May 26, 1961, and she never appeared in court; however, she did deliver the following stipulation:

> *She and Dick met in the fall of 1960, spent time in Paris, and traveled to Tucson where they registered at a hotel under the false name "A.B. Carling." She said Dick paid for everything and gave her $200,000 in jewels, furs, and gifts. In November 1960 she took a trip on the* Rotterdam *with Dick, where they got married in March. She lived on Sapelo afterward and then moved with Dick to Locarno, where they stayed from June till November 1961. While on Sapelo, the sheriff served her and Dick with the subpoena but Dick told her she didn't have to obey it…Annemarie said that Dick gave her additional gifts in excess of $400,000 since November 1960, which included a Mercedes-Benz, a Porsche, stock in her former company, diamonds, and furs…Muriel knew all too well how much Dick spoiled his mistresses…In his closing argument, one of Dick's attorneys concluded his closing arguments with a simple message that Muriel was nothing more than a money-hungry beast. He said: "If ever there was a hen-pecked, devil-driven, hag-ridden poor specimen of humanity it was Mr. Richard Reynolds…during his life with Muriel…This wife as a result of her unholy lust for money has destroyed within herself, within her own breast every symbolance* [sic] *of womanly virtue that she may have had."*

According to author Schnakenberg, divorce proceedings lasted almost four years. During this time, Muriel had spent $500,000 in legal fees, and Dick had spent $1 million, while the court had recorded eight thousand pages of testimony. The jury ruled in Dick's favor after only six hours of deliberation, and they "denied Muriel any alimony whatsoever and revoked the roughly $12,500 per year she was supposed to receive before. The prenuptial agreement would prevail. Muriel was devastated.

What about the bigamy and adultery of Dick Reynolds? This is what he told the court:

> *While they were on the* Rotterdam *cruise, Dick had been cabled by his lawyers that Muriel's motion for a new trial had been denied, so he felt free to marry Annemarie. He moved too quickly…for the marriage to be in "good faith." Dick claimed that since he learned of the divorce decree, he had stopped living with Annemarie as his wife and had been unable*

> *to consummate the marriage due to his illness. Everyone in the courtroom believed this was a lie. After the exhausting trials with Muriel, Dick prepared to leave America.*

Dick Reynolds died about the time Annemarie was due to deliver her first child; consequently, "she gained a beautiful baby girl and lost a new husband she had left everything for—a career, her family, and her own autonomy—just a few years earlier."

"I Don't Want a Sterilize Operation"

According to reporter Kevin Begos, "For more than 40 years North Carolina ran one of the nation's largest and most aggressive sterilization programs. It expanded after World War II, even as most other states pulled back in light of the horrors of Hitler's Germany."

The *Winston-Salem Journal* examined thousands of documents of the state's eugenics board and found the following:

> *More than 2,000 people ages 18 and younger were sterilized in many questionable cases, including a 10-year-old who was castrated. Children were sterilized over the objections of their parents, and the consent process was often a sham.*
>
> *The program had been racially balanced in the early years, but by the late 1960s more than 60 percent of those sterilized were black, and 99 percent were female.*
>
> *Doctors performed sterilizations without authorization and the eugenics board backdated approval. Forsyth County engaged in an illegal sterilization campaign beyond the state program.*
>
> *Major eugenics research at Wake Forest University was paid for by a patron whose long history of ties to science had a racial agenda that included a visit to a 1935 Nazi eugenics conference and extensive efforts to overturn key civil-rights legislation.*

What specifically happened in Winston-Salem? In his book *In the Name of Eugenics*, Daniel Kevles, a professor of history at Yale University, explains:

> *One reason was a group of Winston-Salem's elite who formed the Human Betterment League in 1947. Hosiery king James G. Hanes and Alice*

> *Shelton Gray, a trained nurse and another member of the local elite, joined forces with Dr. Clarence Gamble of Boston, the heir to the Procter & Gamble fortune. The group launched a massive publicity campaign in North Carolina to promote sterilization programs…Hanes and Gamble were concerned about how much welfare mothers and the mentally ill were costing taxpayers.*

The *Winston-Salem Journal* "bought into it, asked a few hard questions, and paved the way for the eugenics board to expand its activities." Publisher of that newspaper Jon Witherspoon apologized for the newspaper's role in legitimizing the "barbaric activities." Witherspoon, on behalf of the *Journal*, apologized for "depriving these individuals of their basic human rights."

The eugenics law, passed in 1929 and amended in 1933, allowed sterilization for three reasons: "epilepsy, sickness and feeblemindedness." In 1945, one woman pleaded with the eugenics board: "I don't want it. I don't approve of it, sir. I don't want a sterilize operation…Let me go home, see if I get along all right. Have mercy on me and let me do that." After giving birth to an out-of-wedlock child, another woman said, "They don't want to hear how I feel, or what's going on in my mind. You're pregnant—you need to get sterilization. And they had the nerve to tell me this was the best thing for me to do."

There were others—"wives and daughters. Sisters. Unwed mothers. Children. Even a 10-year-old boy. Some were blind or mentally retarded."

The grandfather of a seventeen-year-old girl testified at a 1938 eugenics board hearing. These were his words:

> *You are absolutely tearing down the laws of God when you do this. God said when he drove Adam and Eve out of the Garden of Eden—did He tell her to go out and be sterilized? God said go out and multiply. If sterilization isn't against that, what is?*

Just recently, North Carolina became the third state to issue a statement of regret for its sterilization program.

Part IV

Believe It or Not

Board of Censors of Public Amusements

At the March 2, 1917 meeting of the Winston-Salem Directing Board, an ordinance was approved "establishing a Board of Censors of Public Amusements to inspect and view all places of amusement or exhibitions…and to prohibit those, as their judgment, are immoral or against the public interest." Four months later, the July 13 entry read as follows:

> *The question of the power of the Advisory Board composed of ladies of the city, appointed by the Board of Censors, to prohibit or forbid any particular exhibition or part of exhibit which in their judgment is immoral or against the public's interest was discussed and Mr. J.G. Hanes and L.P. Tyree (Aldermen) were appointed a committee to consult with the City attorney in regard to same.*

The next month, at the August 1919 meeting, minutes show that the board approved an ordinance requiring "that all movie theaters submit all films to be exhibited during the following week. It was required that these films be reviewed by the National Board of Review. If a moving picture had not passed the National Board of Review, it could not be shown until approved by the board of aldermen or the board of censors.

That was the last entry concerning censorship, so apparently the National Board of Review was viewing every film before it could be shown in the

Above: Censorship board.

Below: Children looking at posters in front of a movie theater.

Above: Poster for *Black Fury*, a movie about a strike.

Below: Dance hall's bad conditions—a penny picture machine attracting crowds.

movie theater. The board's attention at the May 4, 1917 meeting moved on to dance halls and adopting an ordinance outlawing dance halls where an admission fee was charged. It seems, according to the minutes, that "dance halls had been licensed, under policy scrutiny, since 1914."

SALEM TAVERN—THE PLACE TO DRINK, ARGUE, DUEL

When Brother Jacob Meyer and his wife ran Salem Tavern, "men of all factions and dispositions gathered over tankards of ale and tumblers of good peach brandy, sometimes only to argue and talk and other times to duel with fists and pistols, gouging out eyes and biting off each other's lips." In 1771, at the age of forty-one years, Brother Meyer and his wife arrived to take over management of Salem Tavern.

Only three years after the Revolutionary War, Salem Tavern, according to historians, was "no longer simply a house of entertainment where travelling strangers could find a warm bed, good food and drink, and a hospitable welcome." What visitors found was chaos and terror, and according to historian Hunter James, the environment was not in keeping with the Moravians' utopian idea of what a tavern should be:

> *Even during the best of times, there was uncertainty and disorder; during the worst, chaos and terror. What finer sport than for these drunken militiamen to ridicule the Moravians for their piety while robbing them of their foodstuffs? These were the inevitable consequences of war, particularly in a region still half wild and haphazardly settled. But they were consequences which the Moravian authorities were neither prepared to accept nor able to avoid. To satisfy both the demands of militia officers and the restrictions of the* Aufseher Collegium *posed enormous problems for Brother Meyer. Given the peculiar circumstances of the time, it is perhaps no surprise that he and Sister Meyer grew more careless with their housekeeping and began receiving guests "with bad humor and with grumble."*

Salem Tavern, Winston-Salem, North Carolina.

What transpired next were written reminders to Brother Meyer that he had taken some things for granted, and he was reminded of his duties and obligations:

> *Its ardent desire that the guests who come here (who are of very different dispositions and customs, yea, even occasionally enemies and spies) may be served by our Brother and Sister, in every respect, in such a way that their consciences must tell them that we are an honest and Christian people, such as they have never before found in a tavern; and that this Brother and Sister thus, but their correct conduct, without words, testify to Jesus' death, and in their difficult office and calling, be an honor to the Lord and Congregation.*

So what did the term "correct conduct" mean? According to author Hunter James, these were the rules:

> *All families in Salem shall be obedient to the statues and ordinances of the Congregation, and…keep their servants, both male and female, their children, and strangers, in their proper places.* [The tavern] *would keep good stables, hay, oaks and corn of good quality and abundance…* [and] *good pasture, enclosed with a good fence.* [Likewise,] *the horses of the guests must be fed and properly cared for and the guests themselves must be served with wholesome and plentiful food; also the beer, liquors and wines must be good and unadulterated, and at the same time, the correct weight and measure must be given in every respect…Guests must drink at the bar and not take whisky into their rooms. Meyer would treat all guests with "kindness and cordiality," but would not allow even his most reliable customer to run up a debt in excess of forty shillings…Nor would he countenance card-playing or any other type of gambling.*

And there was more! Brother Meyer was admonished concerning his price of room and liquor, the way he did his bookkeeping, his acceptance of counterfeit currency and the need for him to prevent peddlers from "turning the tavern into a huckstering outlet." In addition, he must always tend to all repairs, be on the alert for suspected wrongdoers and—most importantly—not allow Salem residents to feast and drink in the tavern.

> *It was the growing tendency of the Single Brothers to frequent the tavern at all sorts of hours and under all sorts of circumstances that caused most of the friction between Brother Meyer and the town leaders. Criticism came both from the* Collegium, *which in early 1775 was disturbed over reports that "a*

whole party of Brothers had recently had a gay time in the Tavern," and from the Salem Congregation Council which reminded Meyer that it was his duty "to send those people away"—that the tavern "is for travelling strangers only."

OBEY OUR RULES...OR ELSE

The Salem Cotton Manufacturing, organized on July 9, 1836, consisted of a factory, an engine purchased in Baltimore, necessary spindles and looms and homes for employees. Those who worked in the mill were subjected to the following rules and regulations:

ARTICLE I
No family or individual need apply for employment, without at the same time furnishing certificate from some of their most respectable and trustworthy neighbours, that they are of industrious habits and unexceptional character.

Families that are employed are considered as engaged for as long a time as they and the employer can agree, but are in no case to leave before they have given the employer one month's notice of their intention to do so.

Single individuals are considered as engaged for as long a time as they and the employer can agree, but are in no case to leave before they have given the employer two weeks' notice of their intention to do so.

Any one, that willfully or negligently injures any part of any building or of any machine, will be held accountable for such injury, and the damages deducted from his or her wages.

The working hours in the mill will be from sun-rise until sun-set, from the 20th of March until the 20th of September; and the remaining six months of the year from sun-rise until half past seven, except on Saturday, when the machinery will stop at four o'clock.

ARTICLE II
Persons occupying the family apartments are considered as holding them from week to week, and shall furnish at least five competent hands to work in the factory.

They are to take in as many boarders as they are requested to do by the main superintendent, and to furnish them with plain, wholesome and cleanly food.

They are to keep their houses clean and orderly, and are to permit nothing to be done in the same contrary to the established rules of the place.

They are to take every precaution to guard against fire. They shall not keep their ashes in wooden vessels, nor pour them out on the lot when warm. They shall not carry fire from one house to another in an open vessel, especially when there is any wind. They shall be careful not to let too much soot collect in the chimneys, but burn them out from time to time, during rainy weather.

They shall not permit any of their boarders to leave the house at any unreasonable time, or do any thing that is not strictly according to the established rules.

If the boarders in any manner misbehave, they shall never fail to remind them of their duty.

If their admonitions to such boarders are not regarded, they shall inform the employer of the misconduct of such individuals; and if they fail to do this, they will be considered as encouraging such conduct.

They will be held accountable for any thing done in their families.

Article III

Individuals engaged to attend the different machinery, will repair to their post punctually when the bell calls them to work, and are not to leave the same until the principal machinist stops the mill.

During the working hours they are to act strictly according to the rules of the mills, and the directions given by the superintendents of the rooms in which they are employed.

If they cannot attend from sickness or other cause, they are to acquaint the manager of the fact, and of the cause of the absence.

Unless called away by business, they are to remain at their boarding houses, and after nightfall especially, every one is expected to be at home.

They are not to leave on a visit to any distance without informing the employer of their intention.

Every one is expected carefully to avoid all that may tend to disturb the peace and harmony of persons employed in this establishment.

Every one is expected most strictly to observe the rules of order and morality, as otherwise his or her presence is no longer desirable.

Salem Cotton Manufacturing Company was sold to John Morehead in March 1854. According to one historian, the Mexican War had increased cotton prices, those who purchased manufactured goods could not pay and the mill owed money to suppliers. It seemed to be a lose-lose situation.

$10,000 in Currency Burned

In July 1815, Christian Blum was named agent of Salem's new bank, the Bank of Cape Fear, which had headquarters in Wilmington. In December 1827, disaster struck:

> *He was counting paper currency when it was time to go to the church and light the candles. Leaving bills on the table he hastily blew out the lights, and so far as could be ascertained a spark must have fallen on the paper, for he had hardly reached the church when his table at home was a mass of flames. The fire was put out before the house caught, but an estimated $10,000 in currency was burned.*

Of course, there was an investigation by the Wilmington office; officials there did not believe Blum's story, and he was fired on the spot.

Wickedly Heavy and Dirty Mill Work

Many historians write about mill life in Winston because more and more farm families were moving to the textile mills, and their experiences were often frightening. For twelve to fourteen hours a day at about seventy-five cents a day, men, women and children labored among the noise and movement of the machine. Workers were given about forty-five minutes for lunch. The days were spent "in unpleasant surroundings where lint and dust hung in the air, clinging to the hair and clothes of the operatives, irritating their eyes, and filling their noses and lungs. The clattering of the machinery was all the operatives heard for twelve to fourteen hours a day." In addition, other mill jobs were reported as "unrelenting and often dangerous":

> *The pace was hectic, for the machinery ran with few stops and workers spent the whole day walking among the machinery, reaching, pushing, and pulling as they tended the looms and frames over which they had little control. The reports of the Bureau of Labor Statistics reveal that factory work was unrelenting and often dangerous. Spinners, mostly older children and teenaged women, tended frames of as many as 104 bobbins a side spinning at 5,000 to 10,000 rpm. Experienced spinners tended six to eight sides arranged on each side of an alley through which the spinner walked checking for and quickly piecing together broken threads. Weavers, mostly*

> *older teenagers and young women, had the job that required the most skill in the mill. Working quickly, they adjusted threads on the loom from bobbins and harnesses as warp and woof were woven together into cloth. The fast-paced routing in an environment of exposed running belts and the moving parts of the machines often caused accidents in which mill operatives were seriously injured and maimed.*

Recorded in various historical accounts are serious injuries. One young boy caught his hand in the feed rollers of a wool picker. Others had their hands scalded or burned by sulfuric acid. It is noted that black males perhaps performed the most despicable task: that of "unpacking five-hundred-pound bales of cotton, tearing off chunks of raw cotton to be fed into the picker which cleaned the cotton."

So why did men, women and children flock to the textile mills? The answer: a family with two or three members working in a textile mill could earn an income that easily surpassed what a tenant family could expect. In addition, historians believe that housing in the mill village was a big factor in families staying. Sometimes families were told it was illegal for them to seek employment elsewhere, as evidenced by this letter (printed here as it was written) that T.M. Richardson wrote to Governor Daniel G. Fowle in 1889:

> *Does the laws of the United States or of N.C. or any town in N.C. me as honest laborer who have never been disfranciies, compel a man if he does not owe his implolyer any thing, if he sees where that he can better him self by working for another man in the same town. My only reason to ask you is this, here in Winston N.C. are several tobacco manufacturers and they say it is the law and it have had some great effect on men here.*

Winston-Salem workers ultimately enrolled in the Knights of Labor because they believed that "solidarity and concerted actions" would advance their interests. The Knights of Labor "was founded for the special purpose of assisting the laborers of this land to receive the just fruits of their labor, and a proportionate share of the gains." Consequently, the Knights "united those they believed composed the producing classes—shopkeepers, manufacturers, and skilled, semiskilled, and unskilled workers." This group, according to historians, ultimately came to be regarded as a black organization, and "Nigger and Knight had become synonymous terms."

To working-class whites with uncertain status, workers could easily appear as a threat. Relations between whites and blacks were further complicated as unskilled whites and blacks found themselves in similar circumstances and competing for the same jobs.

Apparently, females had to complete with males for mill jobs. According to historian Michael Shirley, "The proportion of female mill workers in 1880 over age thirty-one was 18 percent." If a widowed women was not employed in the mill, often her children were, as indicated by the following account:

> *The Hanes family was typical. Melissa Hanes, age forty-one and widowed, kept house while three of her children—Emily, eighteen, Mary, fourteen, and Charles, twelve—worked in the mill. Her eldest child, Elizabeth, twenty-five, shared housekeeping duties with her while William, eleven, attended school.*
>
> *Another widow, Elizabeth Bennett, thirty-nine, found security in a company boarding house. John Bennett, sixteen, worked in the mill while Charles, nineteen, worked as a stonecutter. The two youngest children, Lillie, twelve, and Mary, ten, attended school. They shared their household with seven boarders who worked in the Fries mills.*
>
> *The boarding house also contained the household of Eliza Holder, fifty-one, widowed, and a former Salem Manufacturing Company operative. Living with Eliza were two sisters, a nephew, and five boarders.*

Moving from rural farms into town, men, women and children found steady employment; however, they also discovered how a textile mill often necessitated their working long hours in unsafe and backbreaking conditions.

REPEATED PROTESTS

The July 1806 minutes of the Salem Moravian congregation ruling body, *Aufseher Collegium*, reveal a complaint by Brother Ludwig Eberhart and a resolution of the matter:

> *The single* [unmarried] *Br. Joh. Vogler is making silverware. He also is reported to repair clocks, though the Community Direction has granted this work solely to him* [Brother Eberhardt].
>
> *It has to be said against Br. Eberhardt that he does not attend to his work as well as Vogler, also that he often does not make these things at all and otherwise is too high in his prices. The Collegium therefore permits Joh. Vogler to make silverware and repair clocks besides his own profession.*

John Vogler House, 700 South Main Street, Winston-Salem, North Carolina.

According to an article entitled "History Corner: John Vogler (1783–1881) Silversmith of Old Salem" by Silvio A. Bedini, Eberhardt was not satisfied with the *Aufseher Collegium*'s decision; he kept complaining. Several years passed, and Vogler "achieved the status of master craftsman in his own right." The January 25, 1809 minutes reveal the ruling body's action:

> *For a long time Br. John Vogler has had the desire to attend to his business as watchmaker and silversmith in the Brothers' House. There seems to be an opportunity for him now and we discussed the possibility of an objection in the Collegium to his intention. We did not know anything that could be an obstacle to his plans, since he promised not to deal with wall clocks, which is Br. Eberhardt's business alone.*

Until he was an old man, Brother Eberhardt repeatedly protested Vogler's production of various products. Apparently, nothing came of these protestations because John Vogler went on to become Salem's master silversmith.

NO UNIONS!

At the October 12, 1943 board meeting, officials of Winston-Salem responded to a letter from the Congress of Industrial Organization. Members made quite clear their opinions, responding with the following resolution:

> *There is no requirement that the City of Winston-Salem recognize any labor organization as a bargaining agency or otherwise…It is in the best interest of the City of Winston-Salem that no labor organization ever be recognized as a bargaining agency or representation of any employees of the City of Winston-Salem. The Finance and Public Works Committees recommend that the City of Winston-Salem refuse to recognize any labor union or labor organization as a bargaining agency or representative of any employees of the City of Winston-Salem.*

That response just about covered every possible way of saying "no thanks." At the October 26, 1943 meeting, Mayor Coan commented on the resolution by saying, "There has been right much in the papers recently; consequently, he reaffirmed that while no labor union would be recognized, "city employees may talk to City Authorities at any time and be received in a friendly spirit."

WINSTON OFFICERS RAID DISTILLERIES

On August 2, 1899, twelve revenue officers returned to Winston from a big raid in Stokes County. They accomplished their mission when they destroyed eight distilleries belonging to Hill Smith and Jim Taylor, "two of the most noted blockaders in North Carolina." According to a newspaper report, this is what transpired:

> *The officers anticipated trouble and were cautious about entering the distilleries until prepared to get the "drop" on the blockaders. The cause for alarm was on account of the fact that Taylor and Smith have been in several shooting scrapes with revenue men. They were not given a chance to shoot this time. Smith's father, who is quite old, was so drunk that the officers did not interfere with him. A daughter of the old man thanked the officers for their effort in trying to break up the objectionable business.*

The dozen revenue officers destroyed several hundred gallons of beer and whiskey and arrested and jailed Taylor and Smith. The last sentence of the newspaper article refers to Jim Taylor's wealth and anticipates that he would be able to afford bond.

"They Take All the Pie"

In an open letter published in an October 5, 1898 newspaper, *Dinkins Hariston*, a "Winston negro politician" wrote the following message:

> *Now I will say this much to the bosses: You can cheat us out of the primary in Salem Chapel, but if you keep James Carter on that ticket in the place of James Lancar, colored, you will find the colored people voting with the old-time Republicans, the party that has recognized the colored man. I am*

Negro holding a Democratic ticket over a ballot box.

Racist poster attacking Radical Republican opponents of black suffrage.

> *now more surprised at that convention than ever, as "Mr. Boss Reynolds" told me that morning that they had done so much for the negro; said that they had put over three hundred of them in office in this State and said that the Democrats had not given them a single office; but we do not expect any office from the Democrats. We have not been voting with them, or rather they have been voting with us, as the Republican party in this country and State is ours; we do not vote with the white Republicans, they vote with us and take all the pie, as they say.*

BIG HUDSON SIX TURNS OVER THREE TIMES

The date was June 12, 1918, and the newspaper caption read: "Nine Hurt in Auto Wreck." Estes Hairston and all the occupants of the Hudson Six were residents of Winston-Salem. The opening sentence read: "Nine negroes were more or less seriously hurt in an automobile wreck due to fast driving and a blowout. This is what happened, according to the report:

> *The only wonder is that the whole bunch were not killed outright, as the car, a big Hudson Six, turned completely over three times in the road, and people who live near the place say the car was running with throttle wide open. The maximum speed of these cars is said to be above sixty miles an hour. Added to this was the fact that the car had been coming down a slight grade for a hundred yards before it turned over. It is thought that the driver*

Hudson Super Six automobile.

> *of the car jammed on the brakes when the blow-out occurred. The top was up and part of the occupants were hurled through this, while it kept others in the car and two were underneath the wreckage when it stopped rolling. One woman, the doctor thought, had a broken back. Another was thought to be dying when placed in one of the two ambulances sent from Winston-Salem. At noon yesterday none had died; however, four were very seriously hurt, four were able to go home when they got back to Winston-Salem.*
>
> *An empty whiskey flask was found lying near the wreckage.*

So what about the ninth victim? He reportedly "tied up his scalp wound and proceeded to the dance" to which all folks were originally headed.

Somebody Could Get Killed!

Discussion at the August 5, 1949 meeting of the board focused on a block of Second Street, dubbed "the narrowest street in Winston-Salem." The reason Second had not been widened as had other downtown streets went back years, to when the mayor, who lived there, strenuously objected. Alderman Lancaster made the following observation:

> *I understand that the Police Department has authorized that this street be widened, and it is a very dangerous proposition. You take some of these ABC advocates out all Saturday night coming down there Sunday Morning meeting somebody going to church, it might cause an accident and get somebody killed. There has been a person killed on Second Street. By the way, it was a Superintendent of a Sunday School that killed him.*

Mayor Kurfees responded with this statement, "He evidently wasn't coming from an ABC store."

Part V

Straight from the Horse's Mouth

A Deplorable State of Affairs

The date was September 10, 1921, and the newspaper caption read, "Stokes Sheriff Fined $50 for Being Drunk." The man on trial was Sheriff E.O. Shelton, of Stokes County. He was fined ten dollars and costs in the Municipal Court at Winston-Salem on charge of "intoxication and flourishing a pistol at the fair grounds last night." The officers making the arrest testified as follows:

> *They found a pint bottle nearly half full of whiskey on Shelton. In commenting on the case, Judge Hartman declared that a* deplorable state of affairs *is created when the chief officer of a county goes out and violates the law he is sworn to uphold. Judge Hartman also referred to the case of Deputy Sheriff Watson Joyce, of Stokes, who was convicted several months ago of transporting whiskey to Winston-Salem. He also called attention to Judge Long's action in the Superior Court of requiring Joyce to surrender his badge.*
>
> *In reply to an appeal from Sheriff Shelton's lawyers not to impose a fine, Judge Hartman replied that he had no idea of imposing sentence on poor unfortunates, as long as he sat on the bench, and then permit an important officer to go unpunished! He felt like the offense justified a road sentence, but he was willing to give any man a chance.*

A poor man loaded with mischief or matrimony.

Sheriff Shelton gave notice of appeal to the Superior Court. His bond was set at $150. He paid the fine. This case drew a great deal of discussion and speculation about Sheriff Shelton's future when Stokes County commissioners reviewed it.

HAND OVER YOUR MONEY, OR ELSE!

The date was January 26, 1949, and the front-page headline read, "County Boys Charged with Robbery, Bond $2,000 Each." The youths were Owen Lambert and Howard Martin, both nineteen, of Winston-Salem, Route 5, and they were both jailed on charges of robbery with firearms and a knife. Bond was placed at $2,000 each. Lambert and Martin allegedly attacked Eugene Baity, thirty-two, of Winston-Salem on the old Gum Tree Road. The newspaper gives these details:

> *Martin is said to have cut Baity in the palm of his hand with a knife and later to have made threats of shooting him if he did not surrender money, Baily told Forsyth County officers who investigated the case and then turned*

> *it over to the Davidson County sheriff's office. Lambert pressed some object in his back after Martin is alleged to have threatened the shooting. Martin is then said to have taken $12.50 from his pockets. Deputy H.C. Koonts of Davidson County, said Forsyth officers turned the case over to the sheriff's department here after it was found that the alleged incident had happened in Davidson. He said he saw Baity yesterday on a visit to Winston-Salem to pick up the two young men and the man did have a scar in his hand but there was no indication of any serious cut.*

Baity's testimony to arresting officers focused on the events preceding the alleged robbery. He said that Lambert and Martin picked him up near a theater in Winston-Salem and offered to drive him home. Baity said he was driven to several beer joints in Winston-Salem, and there was talk of a visit to a Davidson County bootlegger. He said he did not drink anything at the beer joints, and the visit to the bootlegger was culled after he refused to give the other two any of his money. Of course, it was in Davidson where the alleged robbery was supposed to have occurred. Written statements by Lambert and Martin indicated an entirely different scenario:

> *Lambert said he and Martin had picked up Baity and a round of beer joints was made with all men drinking some beer. He said the visit to a bootlegger was suggested but no whiskey was ever purchased. He said Martin and Baity got out of his car on Gum Tree Road and he heard some remarks by Martin, including a statement by Baity to "turn him loose" and one by Martin, "Did I cut your hand?" but thought the men were just picking on each other. He said he later drove Baity back to Winston-Salem, letting him out of the auto near a car-line. He said on the way back to Martin's home the other man told him he did get $12. He said he asked Martin if he borrowed it and the other man did not reply.*

No other news reports appeared concerning this case. After bond for each case was placed at $2,000, a hearing in county court was expected for Wednesday of the next week.

Sex in the Twin City

In his book *The Gilded Leaf*, Patrick Reynolds, grandson of R.J. Reynolds and a son of Dick Reynolds by his second wife, Marianne O'Brien, takes readers inside the Reynolds family and fortune. Perhaps his most intriguing chapters focus on his grandfather, R.J. Reynolds, and his sexual activities. In Patrick's own words, "R.J. liked fast horses and loose women," as illustrated here:

> *To tickle his lady friends—who were generally poor whites or blacks from his factories rather than the demure daughters of the prosperous—he named new brands of chew after them. Men chewed tobacco for pleasure, not out of duty.*
>
> *R.J. did not lack for female companionship. He used his power as an employer to induce women from the packing floor to come to a back room with him. Often, after having sex with such a partner, he'd return to work.*
>
> *No self-respecting male was supposed to abstain, else he might become ill. Also, a long tradition in the South cast a benevolent eye on white men having intercourse with black women; such coupling and the issue from it were it was a common practice. In this era, sex was considered necessary for a man's health, whether or not he was accepted before the war by white plantation women and after it by white townswomen. Dozens of mulatto and even some white children in Winston in the latter quarter of the nineteenth century learned they were the bastard children of R.J. Reynolds.*
>
> *Men like R.J. were often hesitant to marry upstanding white women of class until they had reformed and cleansed their systems so that the marriage would lead properly to the production of healthy children. Historian Robert Lacour-Gayet has concluded that Southern men's common practice of delaying marriage until their forties or even fifties was attributable to the widespread patronage of black concubines. R.J. liked his wild life—and, year after year, put off marriage.*

According to Patrick Reynolds, his grandfather was "a man of many vices"; he gives the following specifics to illustrate his statement:

> *R.J. was much respected for supplying friends with moonshine: with the cooperation of the owners of a local livery stable, he brought in "brandy" from farmer-distillers in the hills, at several hundred gallons per order.*
>
> *R.J.'s breeding was occasionally in evidence as he squired young white women to the roller-skating rink or attended "occasions" given in a local mansion built by a decorator and festooned with murals of allegorical travels and cupids—but he was more comfortable in less refined pursuits and surrounds. He drank many of his friends and rivals under the table and was a participant in poker games that sometimes lasted day and night through entire weekends. Once a whole factory was at stake on the table.*

R.J. was a man who would bet on anything: whether it would rain on Tuesday, whether a young lady could be bedded. Once, a small boy in Bristol saw R.J. and Ben Parlett walking down a street and followed them. First the men decided to flip coins, and they bet ten-dollar gold pieces. R.J. won. Continuing on, the men bet on who could pull out the longest straw from a hay wagon. Parlett won. Walking farther, they saw two blackbirds sitting on a telegraph wire and bet on which bird would leave the wire first; when both flew together, the men finally ended the betting spree.

Joshua Coin—Blessing or Curse?

When war was declared in 1917 and some of the workers in the R.J. Reynolds Tobacco Company were drafted, R.J. "solemnly touched his Joshua Coin to their gold coins, tokens, teeth fillings. All those who had been similarly touched by the totem in the Civil War and the Spanish-American War had survived; R.J. hoped the coin's magic would still be potent."

The Joshua Coin had been around a long time before R.J. Reynolds inherited the legendary good-luck charm. According to Patrick Reynolds, this good-luck totem had an interesting history:

It had been named for Joshua Cox. Red-haired, six foot six, Joshua Cox had been exiled from England in the 1750s for stealing one of the king's mistresses. During the French and Indian War he'd been captured by a native tribe but spared death because of his unusual physique. After residing with the chief for some time, Cox escaped to civilization by swimming many miles in a river, wearing little but the square Joshua Coin around his neck. The face of the coin showed the stamp of Peruvian imprint of the seventeenth century. Cox believed the coin had saved his life, and it became a totem passed down from generation to generation together with a magic phrase to be said over it.

Touched to a man's gold, the Joshua Coin would bring good fortune. However, for it to work it had to be in the possession of a son in direct descent who bore the name Joshua; if the succession were broached, woe would result. Joshua Cox married late in life, and when he died the totem passed to his son, who also married late. When that son died, the Joshua Coin was passed into the hands of Nancy Jane Cox's second surviving boy, who was probably named after his grandfather in order to receive the totem. He was Richard Joshua Reynolds.

Fifty years later, when R.J. Reynolds and his brother Abram began to amass huge fortunes, rumors spread that the Joshua Coin was one of the original thirty pieces of silver paid to Judas for his betrayal of Christ.

After R.J. Reynolds's death on July 29, 1918, this same Joshua Coin went to the older son, Richard Joshua Reynolds Jr. According to Heidi Schnakenberg in her book *Kid Carolina—R.J. Reynolds Jr.: A Tobacco Fortune and the Mysterious Death of a Southern Icon*, R.J. Reynolds Jr. (Dick) asked Blitz, his ex-wife, to return some of his important items that he had left in Blitz's safe. That meeting did not go well:

> *Of particular importance to him was his pilot's license, his father's Joshua Coin (the ancestral heirloom passed down to male heirs in the family for good luck), and his father's pocket watch and compass, which was an antique nautical navigation timepiece.*
>
> *Blitz had little patience for a man who had left her to raise their children on her own and then suddenly showed up years later to demand his things back. She abruptly stood up and shouted, "You will get nothing back from me! You won't get a single thing out of any of the houses. Not so much as a piece of paper!"*

After Blitz died of cancer in 1961, Dick, "whose health was getting worse, was in need of good luck again." He asked four of his sons to deliver to him the ancestral Joshua Coin. The boys complied with their father's wishes, and when he received the coin, Dick "saw that Blitz had had a diamond placed in it. He became enraged and threw the diamond, and possibly the coin, into the ocean." Apparently, the totem disappeared forever.

SUFFERING IN FORSYTH COUNTY—NO FOOD, NO CROPS, NO MONEY

According to Michael Shirley in his book entitled *From Congregation Town to Industrial City: Culture and Social Change in a Southern Community*, "Until the Confederacy's attack on Fort Sumter the people of Forsyth County remained loyal to the Union"; however, loyalties shifted in this way:

> *Suddenly, though, circumstances changed and events raced toward crisis. The next day, President Lincoln issued his fateful call for seventy-five thousand soldiers to meet the insurrection. Lincoln's action was widely*

> *regarded in North Carolina as coercive and unconstitutional, and the course was fixed. Lincoln's call for troops crystallized public opinion in Forsyth County in support of the Confederate cause.*
>
> *One North Carolinian was "willing to give up my life in defence* [sic] *of my Home and Kindred. I had rather be dead than see the Yanks rule this country."*
>
> *Martha Wilson expressed her fears for her home and family to her friend Julia Jones: "I cannot think the Yankees will whip us in the end but every prospect points toward a lengthy contest and I shudder to think of the trials we will probably have to contend with. I fear our houses will be burnt and our provisions taken from us…may the Lord avert it and give us brave arms and stout hearts to continue to bear all."*

The war brought difficult times for the people of Winston and Salem. Hardships endured for citizens:

> *The army drained the county of its farmers, artisans, and laborers. Wartime economic policies and the decline in industrial and agricultural production led to shortages and inflation which made life more difficult for those remaining at home. The political policies of the Confederate government soured morale and fed disaffection. Within eighteen months, the enthusiasm and confidence that had greeted North Carolina's secession had given way to war-weariness, bitterness, and outright disloyalty.*

Winston-Salem women, children and old men planted crops, but they could not grow enough food. Although the Forsyth County Court of Pleas and Quarter Sessions tried, for a while, to provide soldiers' families with assistance, their efforts were halted when the need became larger than the budget, and payments were discontinued. The Board of Sustenance then received assistance applications from families in dire need. In 1863–64, this board spent about "$192,359 to assist 1,568 wives or children of Forsyth County's soldiers."

People left at home needed clothing and food. Crop failures resulted from "untimely freshets which flooded meadows and a continued drought in the latter part of the crop season." Soldiers sometimes deserted when they learned of the hardships their families were experiencing.

> *J.C. Zimmerman wrote of one soldier whose wife "wrote to him that her children was* [sic] *crying for bread and she had not a mouthful to give them*

> *nor a cent of money." The situation was made worse by the fact that the army would not pay the soldiers so that they could send home a few dollars. Confederate soldiers regularly wrote home advising their wives in matters related to setting out a crop and keeping the farm productive so that their families might survive. While away in the army, Zimmerman remained involved in the operation of his farm, advising his wife when and how much to plant, and how much a day laborer should cost to help her around the farm. Zimmerman's letters to his wife reveal the detailed attention soldiers away from home paid to their farms. In one letter Zimmerman gave his wife specific instructions regarding the farm:*
>
> *"I think if you could sow some wheat it would be best even if you had to give a dollar in one day a good hand ought to put in a bushel or more a day. If you can see how your going to get wheat cheaper another year than to raise it is more than I can see…a hand ought to sow six bushels a week and if it was to come good it ought to make forty or fifty bushels and it would cost six dollars to have it sown this fall…I should like to know how you are saving fodder and how the meadow was whether you had any of it cut…I want you to butcher and sell what cattle you cannot keep this winter…if I do not get to come home next spring to make a crop we will be entirely broke up."*

The war brought social disorder to both Winston and Salem. In the winter of 1893, the *People's Press* reported the "extensive number of fires, to warn town officials to bolster the night patrols—too much caution cannot be exercised in these times to guard against fires and robberies." The newspaper also asked for "dependable policemen" because "property is evidently not as secure as formerly, judging from the frequent robberies." Riots occurred, like this one in April 1865:

> *The F. and H. Fries mill and warehouse were broken into by Stoneman's troops. As Union soldiers opened the doors, a "mob" which had gathered rushed into the factory, not only taking finished goods, but also cutting down cloth still on the looms and cutting the belts which drove the machinery as well. The mob consisted of "all kinds of folks, reputable and disreputable—men, women, and children." Much of the mill property was found in the possession of persons John Fries thought were "good and friendly neighbors."*

The Greatest Catastrophe

According to Mary C. Wiley in "Glimpses of Small-Town Winston," the greatest catastrophe that happened in Winston was when the brick and cement city reservoir burst and the entire northern wall was swept away. This happened about five o'clock on the morning of Wednesday, November 2, 1904. According to Ms. Wiley:

> *The surging torrent of 180,000 gallons of water rushed east and then north following the ravine to Belo's Pond, carrying death and destruction in its path. Eight houses were swept away, the personal effects of the families living in them scattered everywhere. Nine persons were killed and numbers injured more or less seriously. The fire bells rang and the firemen of both towns rushed to the scene of destruction to render heroic voluntary service.*
>
> *Among the people living near the reservoir who miraculously escaped death were a Negro man and his wife. They were carried safely in their bed on the crest of the flood to the bottom land around Belo's Pond. A boy whose mother was crushed to death in the collapse of the wall was saved because the bed on which he was sleeping was in an upper room under the roof, where the two sides came together in a peak; when the large stones hit the house, the low roof dropped over the bed, permitting the sleeping boy to continue his nap in safety.*

Possibly the one good thing concerning this catastrophe was the fact that just ten days earlier, Winston's new water plant was up and running. This prevented the town from being without water because every cistern would have been dry in less than two days.

The Town of Winston Directing Board minutes for a called meeting at 9:00 a.m. on November 2, 1904, indicate that the City Water Reservoir (dam) burst that same morning. Additional details discussed at the board meeting are included in these minutes:

> *The north wall of the reservoir collapsed, demolishing the home of Martin Peoples who lived next door, and emptying about a million gallons of water into the street. The water rushed east down the steep hill at Trade Street and then followed the ravine to Belo's pond.*
>
> *The mighty crash of concrete sounded too much like an earthquake. One man looked out his window to see a huge river coming down the street carrying parts of houses and rubbish. Some people were crushed under the*

> *bricks and stone and some were swept away by the powerful force of the water. A total of eight houses were destroyed.*
>
> *One man escaped injury by clinging to a fence while William Adams and his wife rode out the flood on their mattress, landing safely 500 yards from their home.*
>
> *Several people were swept away from their homes east toward the railroad junction, which was covered with water and debris. When the concrete settled and the water stopped flowing, nine people had been killed and ten injured.*
>
> *Mayor Eaton was authorized to look after the proper preparation and burial of all the dead. Aldermen Norfleet, Lüpfert and Brown, with the Mayor added, were appointed a Committee with power to adjust and make a settlement of all personal property loss and damage claims, and all personal injury and death claims.*

The *Western Sentinel* newspaper called the collapse "the most horrible catastrophe in the history of Winston-Salem." The *Union Republican* termed it "the saddest Chapter in our history." The *Winston-Salem Journal* called it "Winston-Salem's greatest tragedy." Reports also indicate that several thousand people gathered to watch the events of that morning.

"ALL WE ASK IS TO BE LET ALONE"—JEFFERSON DAVIS

Abraham Lincoln.

One historian reminds his readers that citizens of Winston and Salem were loyal to the Union for a while during the Civil War. At an April 12, 1861 meeting, before citizens of Forsyth County received word of the attack on Fort Sumter earlier that day, a Union meeting convened, and those in attendance "resolved that now was the time when the conservative, industrial masses, without reference to their past party association, should also peaceably unite and firmly combine their influence and energies to meet the threatening attempts at revolution and civil strife in this State."

After President Lincoln issued a call to enlist seventy-five thousand soldiers, Forsyth County turned its alliance from the Union to the Confederacy. The rationale was simple: it was "a fight to resist submission to 'the yoke of despotism' which would mean 'servile subjugation and ruin.'"

Carrying out this decision proved to be more difficult than the philosophical explanation; however, Forsyth County citizens of both Winston and Salem answered the call to go to war.

Many important tasks needed to be performed:

> *Two volunteer companies from the Salem vicinity, each numbering fifty men, were organized. One adopted the name of "Forsyth Riflemen" and the other the "Forsyth Grays." As the men of Winston and Salem enlisted, the Winston town commissioners appointed a committee to consult with local gunsmiths on the "practicality of changing the flint muskets now in the possession of the town, into percussion muskets."*
>
> *The woman of the community also rushed into the excitement of mobilization and preparation for war. In Salem the women gathered at the Odd Fellows and Temperance halls to make uniforms and put together other war supplies for the two companies.*

When everything was readied for war, family members said goodbye to their husbands, brothers and fathers and were on their way to fight. Of course, the army had taken men who had been farmers, laborers and artisans. Women and children were forced by necessity to plant the crops. Inflation, droughts and lack of manpower made life "deplorable" for those left at home.

Soldiers did not receive pay for their services, so they could send no money back home. Prices rose significantly: "coffee and sugar each sold for twenty-five center per pound, and bacon from eighteen cents to twenty cents per pound." Riots, lootings, fires and burglaries were practically daily occurrences.

Something had to be done, so on August 26, 1863, hundreds of Winston citizens met "to address the issue of peace and to protest succession and its cost in lives and property." Following is what transpired at that important gathering:

> *The meeting accused those who led the state into secession of demanding "the last man and the last dollar in persistence of their fruitless and destructive policy which has well nigh proved the downfall and ruin of the South." Convinced that continued fighting would bring no solution, the citizens demanded a fair and honorable settlement which would secure their*

> *property. The people believed that the only ones who favored continuing the fight were the "speculator and extortion, and the high paid officers, civil and military, who are fattening on the carnage of war and the destruction of civil and religious liberty." The Civil War indeed marked a watershed for Winston and Salem.*

FIRE BUGS

Winston's first fire company came into being on March 2, 1886, and fire horses served a dual purpose. They were used both for hauling supplies and for answering fire alarms. The *Union Republican* of December 16, 1886, refers to the fire horses in this way: "The town commissioners have erected a stable adjoining the fire house and have two mules quartered there to draw the city garbage cart and in case of fire to draw the fire engine." According to one historian, "It was in the early 1890s that firebugs seemed to be at work in Winston." Here are true examples that support that statement:

> *First in one section of the town and then in another unexplained fires would break out. In the Memorial of Robah B. Kerner, who was mayor during this period, a vivid description is given of one afternoon and evening of terror.*
>
> *While at one fire, the Mayor was summoned by fire bells loud and long to another section of the town. After assisting the volunteer firemen in getting this second fire under control, the Mayor, exhausted from his labors, drove to his home on West Fifth near Summit, but scarcely had he seated himself at the supper table when the fire bells summoned him to a third fire.*
>
> *This time a fire was raging near the Courthouse Square, and the Mayor, hastening to the Square, found a scene of wild confusion. "Firemen ran," says the* Memorial, *"The engines roared, a babel* [sic] *of voices rent the air, and from every warehouse and church steeple bells rang, and all the while the excited populace were rapidly congregating on every corner and every conceivable place.*
>
> *Seeing that great danger was imminent, the young Mayor sprang upon the nearest goods box and lifting his voice like a trumpet called to the seething mass of people: "Disperse! Disperse at once! Anyone remaining on the streets will be immediately sent to jail!"*

The crowds dispersed after the jail threat rang through the smoke, and Winston firemen were better able to put out the fire; consequently, those who

Firefighters.

left apparently slept soundly as policemen walked up and down the streets, making sure all the flames had been extinguished.

Racist Slogans and Ugly Epithets

When fifteen-year-old Gwendolyn Yvonne Bailey became the first black student to enter a white Winston-Salem school, she was greeted with painted racist slogans on the school's circular drive. Students who belonged to R.J.R. service clubs scrubbed away the nasty comments, "while the cameras of *Life*, *Look*, and other national publications clicked away. One historian noted, "The bulk of R.J.R.'s students were more interested in the football team that would go on to be state co-champions."

Dispute Over Who Should Tax Tobacco

On April 1, 1902, the finance committee of the Town of Winston was told to pay $901.13 to settle with the R.J. Reynolds Tobacco Company for 1900 taxes. This edict was in reference to the tobacco company storing tobacco in the town of Salem, although the company had its official office and place of business in Winston. The dispute had been over the question: who could tax the tobacco? A legal opinion rendered by Watson, Buxton and Watson stated, "It seems that Salem has the right to collect the tax on such property as if stored in that town, regardless of where the principal place of business of the R.J. Reynolds Tobacco Company is."

The board also authorized the Finance Committee to sign a contract "guaranteeing and protecting the said company against any loss by reason of any law suit that might be brought by the Town of Salem."

INFAMOUS, COWARDLY AND DASTARDLY ATTACK

On Saturday, September 7, 1901, citizens of both Salem and Winston held a joint meeting at the courthouse to adopt unanimously a resolution concerning the assassination of President William McKinley, who was shot at Buffalo, New York, on September 6, 1901. Following is the resolution as it appeared in the Directing Board minutes:

> *Whereas, an infamous, cowardly and dastardly attack has been made upon the honored President of these United States with an infamous attempt to take his life: Resolved, That we, the citizens of Winston-Salem, N.C., in mass meeting assembled, condemn and in most unequivocal terms denounce the impious act and the would-be assassin.*

Honorable William McKinley, president of the United States.

> *Resolved 2nd, That we desire and approve of such speedy and severe punishment as so great a criminal deserves, and such as will be an object lesson to others.*
>
> *Resolved 3rd, That anarchists and nihilists are a menace to society and good government, and that some law should be enacted under which they can be exiled, imprisoned or prevented from endangering the life, liberty, and the pursuit of happiness in this fair land of ours.*
>
> *Resolved 4th, That we appreciate the goodness and greatness of our honored President, the friendly spirit he has always manifested to the South, and his excellent record in peace and war, and that we devoutly and earnestly pray that his life may be spared.*
>
> *Resolved 5th, That we extend our tenderest and sincerest sympathy to Mrs. McKinley and the family of the President in this hour of great trial and severe affliction.*
>
> *Resolved 6th, That copies of these resolutions be furnished Mrs. McKinley and the press, and that copies be spread upon the minutes of the Boards of Aldermen of both cities, the Chamber of Commerce and other societies and organizations.*

President William McKinley died the same day the board adopted these resolutions.

Cursing and Swearing on the Streets

A January 30, 1895 newspaper article was entitled "They Ran Away." Some of the terminology used in the nineteenth century is interesting, but it is sometimes rather vague, as indicated here:

> *A crowd of small negroes went to a school breaking near the Jersey last week and imbibed too freely of corn juice; consequently when they came back home they were rather boisterous, cursing and swearing on the streets. The next morning, on learning that warrants were out for their arrest, they hit the grit for Winston. One of them drove back from there a few days afterwards, and was arrested and carried before His Honor, Mayor Pennix, who suspended punishment until they could all be arrested. We learn the negroes are at work in the tobacco factories at Winston.*

No subsequent newspaper report indicates whether all were arrested or what transpired next.

Part VI
On the Lighter Side

First Court Case of Its Kind—The Butler Did It!

The *Winston-Salem Journal*, in an October 28, 1919 report, announced a Forsyth County jury awarding $271 to Mrs. J.H. Reich "for damages of an automobile alleged to have been caused by careless driving on the part of the owner's butler." According to the article, this was a first to be tried before any court in the United States. Here are the facts and comments:

> *If the case is taken to the supreme court, it will be the first opportunity given that august body to write a ruling on the scope of the law generally termed "A law defining responsibility of automobile owners." There has been an opinion handed down from the supreme court that an automobile owner is responsible for the negligence of any member of his immediate family, or any authorized agent handling or driving at the request or command of the owner. In the case just concluded, however, it was the contention of the defendant that the butler was using the car for his own personal pleasure, and not for, or at the command or request of the defendant's owner of the car.*

So, according to the article, a question was raised but not answered: did members of the family really mind members of the households using the vehicles?

A chauffeur holds a door open for a lady.

HE SQUEALED ON DADDY'S WHISKEY STASH

Law and moonshine—crooked whiskey in North Carolina.

An August 20, 1919 article focuses on L.O. Spease, a Winston-Salem businessman who was fined $250 in city court for having too much whiskey in his possession. Officers found "nine gallons in his home, but no evidence was discovered that the defendant had offered any of it for sale." Who was responsible for the indictment? That's an interesting postscript, as related here:

It appears, according to a dispatch from Winston-Salem, that Mr. Spease's 12-year-old son was responsible for his indictment. The boy, it seems, had been threatened with punishment by his father for disobedience, and he soon proceeded to put some of the officers wise to the fact that "dad" had a lot of whiskey in his home.

The son's squealing led to the indictment. Guess that means the "squeaky wheel really does get the grease."

Ban the Wicked Circus?

In May 1835, a joint meeting of the *Aufseher Collegium* and Salem's elders was called to make a very important decision:

> *To consider whether, to hinder many disorders, a circus announced for next Thursday in town should be forbidden, if possible. At another place there was something similar, with a show of all kinds of foreign animals by day and a circus at night. At the circus there would probably be all sorts of juggling and unfitting tricks which would injure modesty and lead to immorality and might be detrimental to the character of our town.*

Ringling Bros.

A discussion of the above consideration ensued, according to historical accounts. Some of the comments made at that meeting indicated both pros and cons for banning the show. First, the elders were sure that if the circus were not to be permitted to come to Salem, then the brethren would travel to nearby Waughtown. Perhaps it would be better if the circus were allowed to perform at Salem—that way, the elders could control any "excesses" that might occur.

One council member remembered the same predicament arising in earlier years and made this comment: "Everything went along properly and the circus men, out of respect for our town, did not present improper theatrical scenes." That ended the discussion with the understanding that the tavern keeper, in accommodating the circus people, would make sure the strangers did not "undertake anything unfitting to our town."

CIGARS AND TOBACCO OKAY, BUT NO CIGARETTES ON THE SABBATH!

According to one historical record, chapter 4, section 23, of the city ordinances read in part: "But drug stores may be kept open at all times but no cigars, tobacco, soda water, mineral water, or any goods except for medical purposes shall be sold on the Sabbath at any place within the corporation of the City." This ordinance was changed by a June 5, 1900 Town of Winston Direction Board meeting.

FATHER KNICKERBOCKER'S FIGHT FOR A SENSIBLE SUNDAY LAW.

The Hayseed Legislator and the Temperance Fanatic Must be Disposed of Before he can Abolish Police Blackmail.

Fight for a sensible Sunday law.

A motion was made to amend this section by striking out the words "cigars and tobacco" after the words "but no" and inserting the word "cigarettes." Five aldermen voted for the amendment, and the three other members present voted against the change.

Circus Wagons Do Damage

The September 26, 1913 meeting of the Winston-Salem Direction Board passed the following mandate:

> *Heavy circus wagons have seriously damaged the brick pavement between and on the sides of the street car tracks. Be It Ordained that no circus wagons shall be permitted on any brick paving between or on the outside of any car track of the city of Winston-Salem, N.C. except at street crossings.*

Not on Sunday

Minutes of the August 9, 1918 directing board dealt with Sunday Blue Laws in this way:

> *For Sunday. The Board had disapproved a new ordinance allowing the sale of soft drinks and ice cream. The delivery of ice by ice houses was approved. There are several letters from churches printed in the minutes of this date in favor of the continued strict observance of Sunday as a day or rest. The Mayor was to appoint a committee "to settle the question for all time either by a vote of the citizens or otherwise and to incorporate it in the charter."*

On September 6, 1918, the board amended the earlier ordinance in this way:

> *To permit the sale of cigars, tobacco and tobacco products from 8 until 10 A.M. and from 2 P.M. until 6 P.M. Ice houses and dairies selling milk and cream were to close from 11 A.M. until 3 P.M. Soft drinks still were forbidden to be sold.*

WHO STOLE THE $450?

The date was June 7, 1945, and the front-page headline read, "Twin City Woman Freed on Charge of Larceny Here: Judge Holds Evidence on Who Got $450 on Party as Inconclusive." The incident that brought Miss Connie Martin of Winston-Salem to court began with a party in Winston-Salem, attended by three men and three women, and ended with a trip to Arvel Merritt's garage in Lexington. Arvel Merritt testified, explaining the stop at his garage:

> *The prosecuting witness testified that the group were driving around and that when he discovered his car needed mechanical attention he drove to his garage to make repair. He said he had $1,060 in a roll of bills which he gave to another woman companion to keep while he worked on the car. Further testimony was that the un-named woman handed Miss Martin the purse with the money, and she took it into the rest room, then returned it upon coming out in a short time.*

Merritt said that after his friend returned his roll of bills, he discovered $450 missing. The defendant denied she saw the money. She further added that she was the only one not drinking whiskey, purchased on route, that night—she had taken only beer.

There were several humorous touches to the hearing, not the least of which was the testimony of Miss Martin that she "waked up the morning after the party with the mumps." The judge ruled "no probable cause" in this case, and Miss Martin was a free woman.

IT WAS JUST A BASEBALL GAME!

Brothers Charles and Frank Snipes were arrested by Officer W.A. Byrd following a fight with two members of the Winston-Salem Twins baseball team. Byrd charged him with assault and released him on his own recognizance until his court date. The records indicate that Charles's father, Frank Snipes Sr., "was rather well-to-do having made his money running the slaughterhouse that was on Abattoir Street." The July 26, 1913 Winston-Salem Directing Board gives specifics concerning Charles's arrest:

> *Snipes, according to witnesses had been drinking and was upset over the local team's loss to Durham Friday afternoon at Prince Albert Park.*

Umpire making the call on a man sliding into home plate.

> *Charles Snipes allegedly had a baseball bat under his coat and after the game had scuffled with two members of the Twins. Witnesses said the officers did not try to stop the fight after they got the bat away from Charles Snipes and the fight was finally halted by a baseball association official.*
>
> *Snipes then went home, got a Winchester rifle, at least two of his brothers and several friends and went to the Webster Hotel on Trade Street where the ball team was staying. In the lobby Snipes and at least one member of the Twins, Tiny Stuart, the left-fielder, went at it again.*
>
> *Chief J.A. Thomas and several officers responded to the hotel clerk's call for help and took Snipes outside. He was again charged and sent home. Snipes and eight or ten of his friends returned to the hotel later that evening and started to fight with Stuart again. Sergeant Thompson was there this time. He arrested Snipes and put him under a $500 appearance bond and sent him home.*

At a special called meeting of the board on Saturday night, July 26, 1913, Chief Thomas testified that he did not know what had occurred earlier at the ballpark. He and Byrd were suspended "pending a complete investigation by the Police Committee." Then, Sergeant Thompson was suspended for five days without pay because he had failed to jail Snipes. The Snipes brothers received "time on the road gang," and fines were issued to the baseball players. Chief Thomas was soon reinstated when he admitted his mistake by not jailing Snipes. Officer Byrd resigned. A newspaper report indicated that approximately eight hundred local citizens attended these proceedings, "the matter of which stirred the city to its very foundation…the Aldermen have written the word *finis* across the face of the matter and it will drop into the forgotten past in a few weeks."

HOW DARE YOU?

Zelma Kathryn Elisabeth Hedrick was born in Winston-Salem, North Carolina, on February 9, 1922, to Charles E. Hedrick, a building contractor and realtor, and his wife, Lillian Grayson Hedrick. When Zelma Kathryn Elisabeth was twelve-years-old, the family moved to St. Louis, Missouri, where she was discovered "singing on the empty stage of the St. Louis Municipal Opera House, by a janitor, who introduced her to Frances Marshall of the Chicago Civic Opera. Marshall subsequently gave the girl voice lessons." Moviegoers would recognize her stage name: Kathryn Grayson. In 1950, Grayson, portraying an opera singer in *The Toast of New Orleans*, costarred with tenor Mario Lanza. That went well; however, later, while shooting *Madame Butterfly* with Lanza, Grayson had to go to wickedly drastic means to keep Lanza from "attempting to French kiss her." This is what she did to remedy his unwanted advances:

> *Lanza kept attempting to French kiss Grayson, which Grayson claimed was made even worse by the fact that Lanza would constantly eat garlic before shooting. Grayson went to costume designer Helen Rose and she sewed pieces of brass into Grayson's gloves. Any time Lanza attempted to French kiss her after that, she hit him with the brass-filled glove.*

Apparently, Grayson's defensive measures worked, and although Kathryn Grayson's career was extensive and productive—without Mario Lanza—she was offered $10,000 in 1952 to perform at the Riviera Club in New Jersey. Grayson died in her sleep at her California home in 2010. She was eighty-eight years old.

Five-Dollar Fines for Not Using "Soft Paper"

The Town of Winston Directing Board must have had a slow month in July 1902. It set forth this new ordinance: "Be it ordained—that any person who shall be found guilty of using any other material than soft paper in any water closet connected with the City Sewer lines shall be fined $5.00 for each offense."

Wonder how board members knew whom to fine? And also how many offenses? Were there newly appointed toilet paper policemen?

Relatives Need Not Apply

The board made this June 4, 1915 written declaration: "No person shall be appointed or elected by the Board of Aldermen to an office or position in any of the Departments of the City who is related by blood or marriage to the Mayor, a member of the Board of Aldermen, or head of any of the different departments of the City."

Wicked Arithmetic

In his book entitled *Salem: Star and Dawn*, Ernest McNeill Eller writes of education for little girls "in the blossoming month of April 1772, located in the Gemein (Congregation) House." This was home for the pastor and the place where all religious services were held before a church was erected. It was also where the single sisters and older girl choirs resided, because "the people of this land are rude" and the sisters "would be exposed to insolence by day and night. To be in the same house with the minister and his wife gives them protection."

Teacher Sister Oesterlein made a little over sixty cents per week and was obviously completely satisfied until the following events unfolded:

> *Arrangements should be made to give our little girls lessons in arithmetic. Sr. Oesterlein has taught them reading and writing, sewing and knitting, with good success, and that arithmetic has been lacking is only because the Sister knows none. Sr. Oesterlein apparently preferred taking a chance at marriage to learning the complexities of arithmetic. Scarcely 4 months later, in the spring of 1780—a leap year—she passed on the school to a successor and became a bride.*

Girls in arithmetic class.

ORDINANCES: FIRE, CENSORSHIP AND WHISTLING

Although today we probably do not think that overcrowding at a concert hall would be a big issue, the Town of Winston devoted a great deal of time and energy to developing fire ordinances for the Elks Auditorium on the corner of Fifth and Liberty Streets. Board minutes for the February 4, 1904 meeting enacted ordinances directly related to the structure. They included the following items:

> *That admission to the Auditorium shall be limited to seating capacity provided; That when necessary standing room on the first floor only may be permissible. No chairs were allowed in the aisles and management was to provide a man at every exit door. It is further required of the management that extra caution is to be observed at every matinee or day performance as an assemblage at such time is largely composed of ladies and children. That no person present at any entertainment or performance shall be permitted to indulge in any unnecessary noise by whistling or otherwise rendering themselves disagreeable to the audience or performers.*

Obey This Ordinance or Pay the Fine

The February 2, 1905 minutes of the Town of Winston Directing Board voted on the following new ordinance:

> *All property owners or occupants of property fronting on or surrounded by sidewalks within the business district of the City of Winston, be required to remove all snow and sleet from such sidewalks and that the work be completed by 8:30 o'clock A.M. when the precipitation is at night, and immediately after or during the precipitation if the same interferes materially with pedestrians.*

If anyone violated this ordinance, that property owner or store occupant would be fined five dollars.

No Weeds, Spitting, Loitering or Garbage in the Street

The Board of Winston passed this ordinance at the July 2, 1903 meeting:

> *All persons residing in the City of Winston, shall be and are required to keep the sidewalks in front of their premises in a clean condition and shall regularly remove all grass and weeds therefrom* [sic]. *Anyone violating provisions of the ordinance shall be fined $1.00 for each offense.*

On July 7, 1904, the directing board for the Town of Winston passed a series of ordinances dealing with conduct at the station. These included loitering in the reception room and spitting on the floor or furniture.

The board voted on refuse collection (the beginning of backyard collection of household refuse in the residential sections) within the town at the March 1, 1906 meeting: "All trash deposits in Sections of the City, not within the fire limits, shall not be placed on the streets but deposited on the premises until removed by the City trash wagons."

Winston Court Has Difficult Case

A March 14, 1900 newspaper article focuses on a Winston court with a judge, a jury, seven lawyers and thirty-nine witnesses "engaged for four whole days

Jury.

deciding to whom a $4 hog belonged." Commentary follows concerning the case: "No danger of losing liberty in a country as free as this. The humblest gets his rights. This $4 now stands for the right of property, which is always held sacred here in North Carolina."

This snippet is all readers get. There is no mention of who owned the hog.

THIN, PUNY AND LETHARGIC

Newspapers in the Winston and Salem area published many advertisements with personal tributes recommending this or that over-the-counter remedy for almost any ailment. One particular remedy called Dreco seemed to be a magic cure for lethargy, as R.I. Lewis of RFD #3, Winston-Salem, witnesses here:

> *My little son, Verney, was in a terribly run-down condition. He has always been a puny and delicate child and I couldn't get anything to make him grow. But Dreco has hit the spot and he is improving wonderfully every day. His color is good, appetite fine, and I can almost see him grow. It has made him as spry as a rabbit and I told him the other day I would have to slow him up as he was acting too alive.*

Rohrer's bitters advertisement.

The rather lengthy advertisement explains that after schools have dismissed for the summer months, children and young people suffer from the "exhaustive brain work" they have endured during the school year. Teachers, parents and scholars need a tonic like Dreco—which "feeds the brains and nerves and enriches and purifies the blood"—to make boys and girls feel well and strong. Furthermore, this tonic does its curative work in a simple, straightforward way and works quickly to strengthen the weak and "fully restore lost nerve source." Because the advertisement reads as an article, no mention is made of supplier or cost.

He Stole a Suitcase and Wore the Clothes

A September 18, 1912 newspaper article concerned Arthur Boyd, "colored, who was wanted for stealing a suitcase and some clothes, the property of another negro employed at Dall Mountain." When a deputy sheriff attempted to make an arrest, Boyd escaped, but he was ultimately arrested by the Twin Cities police.

Boyd had the suitcase in his possession at the time of his arrest and was said to even be wearing some of the clothes. The news release also revealed that had been jailed pending his trial.

Strong Opposition to Sunday Movies

At the September 29, 1941 meeting of the City of Winston-Salem's Directing Board, opposition to "lifting a ban on Sunday movies for the benefit of soldiers in the city as a result of military maneuvers," came in the form of verbal objection from the Men's Bible Class of the Fourth Street Church of Christ, Friends Church, Central Terrace Methodist Church, Burkehead Methodist Church, Calvary Moravian Church, George W. Lee Memorial Presbyterian Church, First Evangelical and Reformed Church and North Winston Baptist Church. The ordinance passed.

Halloween Celebration Canceled, but Dog Races OK

Winston-Salem's annual City Halloween celebration was cancelled, "having to do with civilian defense, rationing of tires and gasoline, and the regulation of transportation." The minutes of the Directing Board of October 16, 1942, indicate that "this action [was] not to interfere with the celebration of Halloween in the homes and local neighborhoods throughout the residential sections of the City." Interestingly, at that same meeting, the Junior Chamber of Commerce was granted permission to hold dog races in the city on October 29–30 to raise money toward "War Projects."

Couple at the races.

Appendix

Recipes Probably Served in Old Winston and Old Salem

Tunnel of Fudge Cake

1¾ cups butter
1¾ cups sugar
6 eggs
2¼ cups all-purpose flour
¾ cup cocoa powder (not mix)
2 cups chopped walnuts (do not omit or use less)

Glaze
¾ cup powdered sugar
¼ cup cocoa powder
3 to 4 tablespoons milk
¼ teaspoon vanilla flavoring

Cream butter and sugar until light and fluffy. Add eggs one at a time, beating well after each addition. Add flour gradually, mixing with a spoon. Sift powdered sugar and cocoa and add to batter along with walnuts; stir well. Pour into a greased and floured Bundt or 10-inch tube pan and bake in a preheated 350-degree oven for 45 to 50 minutes.

Remove and cool in pan for 45 minutes, then on a rack for two hours.

To make glaze, sift sugar and cocoa, then mix with milk and flavoring until smooth, adding more milk if necessary. Spoon onto cooled cake.

Chicken in Puff Pastry

1 small onion diced
1 tablespoon chopped garlic
1 tablespoon butter
1 ¼ pounds diced chicken
¾ cup heavy cream
1 cup half and half
1 teaspoon Dijon mustard
1 tablespoon tarragon
¾ cups green peas
Salt and pepper to taste
6 frozen puff pastries

Sauté onion and garlic in butter until softened. Add chicken and brown lightly. Stir in cream, half and half, mustard, tarragon, and peas. Mix well and bring to a heavy simmer, stirring often to prevent sticking. Continue simmering until thickened. Add salt and pepper. Scoop mixture into a warm puff pastry and add a little sauce over the top.

Fresh Strawberry Ice Cream

1 quart fresh strawberries, mashed, or 2 packages (16 ounces each) frozen whole, unsweetened strawberries, thawed and mashed
1½ cups sugar
2 tall cans (13 fluid ounces each) evaporated milk
1 tablespoon lemon juice

NOTE: To mash berries, place in blender container and blend until pureed.

Mix together mashed strawberries and sugar. Stir in evaporated milk and lemon juice. Refrigerate until well chilled. Pour into a 2-quart ice cream freezer container. Churn and freeze according to manufacturer's directions. Makes 2 quarts.

To make without an ice cream freezer: Pour 1 tall can of evaporated milk into large mixing bowl. Freeze until ice crystals form along the edges. Beat chilled mixture until foamy. Mix in ¾ cup sugar, 1 pint fresh strawberries, mashed (or 1 16-ounce package frozen whole, unsweetened strawberries, thawed/mashed), and 2 teaspoons lemon juice. Beat until the mixture doubles in size. Pour into 9-inch-square baking pan. Freeze until firm. Makes about 1 ½ quarts.

Potato Casserole

8–9 baking potatoes, boiled and peeled
¼ cup hot milk
2 3-ounce packages cream cheese

1 cup sour cream
2 tablespoons butter
2 teaspoons onion salt
1 teaspoon salt
¼ teaspoon pepper
Butter to dot
Paprika

Cream potatoes with hot milk; add the rest of the ingredients and put in a 2-quart buttered casserole dish. Dot with butter and sprinkle paprika over top. Bake at 350 degrees until bubbly. Serves 10 to 12.

Scalloped Oysters

1 cup bread crumbs
2 cups cracker crumbs
1 cup butter, melted
1 quart oysters
Salt and pepper to taste
4 tablespoons cream
¾ to 1 cup oyster liquor

Examine oysters for shells. Combine bread and cracker crumbs and mix with melted butter. Put a thin layer in the bottom of a dish and cover with a layer of oysters. Season with salt and pepper. Add half of cream and oyster liquor. Repeat and cover the top with the remaining crumbs. Bake for 30 minutes at 450 degrees.

Homemade Ol' Timey Pimento Cheese

1 5.3-ounce can evaporated milk
1 pound sharp cheddar cheese, grated
1 egg
8 ounces pimento, drained and finely chopped
½ teaspoon salt
¼ teaspoon dried mustard
⅛ teaspoon cayenne pepper
⅛ teaspoon Worcestershire sauce
½ teaspoon garlic salt
½ teaspoon onion salt

Heat the milk in the top of a double boiler, add the cheese and stir until it has melted. Remove from the stove and add one well-beaten egg, the pimento and all the spices. Set aside to cool; cover and refrigerate.

Homemade Mayonnaise

Beat together with rotary beater:

1 egg yolk
1 teaspoon mustard
1 teaspoon confectioners' sugar
¼ teaspoon salt
Dash of cayenne pepper
1 tablespoon lemon juice

Continue beating while adding the following, at first drop by drop and then gradually increasing the amount as mixture thickens until all is used up:

1 cup salad oil

Slowly add:
1 more tablespoon lemon juice
Beat well. Chill before serving. Makes about 1½ cups.

Chicken and Corn Chowder

Place the neck, wings, back pieces and giblets of a fat hen in a kettle with the following:

1½ quarts boiling water
1 sliced onion
3 stalks of celery (with leaves), chopped fine
1 carrot, diced
1 tablespoon salt

Cover and simmer until tender (about 1½ hours). Slip meat from bones, cut it up fine and return to broth. Add:
2 cups cream style corn
Simmer for 10 minutes and then add:
2 hard-cooked eggs, chopped fine
Drop rivels into soup and simmer for 10 minutes.

Rivels
Work 1 egg into 1 cup flour and ¼ teaspoon salt, sifted together until mixture looks like corn meal. Drop into boiling soup.

Welsh Rarebit (Welsh Rabbit)

Melt over hot (not boiling) water 4 cups sliced "nippy" American cheese (about 1 pound).

NOTE: Never allow cheese to reach boiling point.

Gradually stir in the following:

¾ cup cream
½ teaspoon dry mustard
½ teaspoon Worcestershire sauce
¼ teaspoon salt
Dash of black pepper

Serve at once on toast.

Deluxe Macaroni and Cheese

1 8-ounce package elbow macaroni
2 cups cream-style cottage cheese
1 cup sour cream
1 slightly beaten egg
¾ teaspoon salt
Dash of pepper
2 cups shredded cheddar cheese

Cook macaroni according to package directions and drain. Combine cottage cheese, sour cream, egg, salt and pepper. Add shredded cheese, mixing well; stir in cooked macaroni. Turn into greased 9- by 9- by 2-inch baking dish. Bake at 350 degrees for 45 minutes.

Candied Yams

8 medium sweet potatoes
1 cup sugar
1 cup water
1 teaspoon vanilla
1 cup brown sugar
2 tablespoons flour
1 stick butter
½ teaspoon nutmeg or cinnamon

Cook potatoes until tender. Peel and slice into baking dish. In saucepan, blend sugars and flour; stir in water. Add butter, vanilla and nutmeg or cinnamon. Bring to a boil and pour over potatoes. Bake at 350 degrees for 30 minutes, basting with syrup.

FRIED GREEN TOMATOES

6 medium-sized fresh green tomatoes, cut into ¼-inch slices
1½ cups buttermilk
1 cup cornmeal
½ cup unbleached flour
1 tablespoon salt
1½ teaspoons cayenne pepper
2 teaspoons dried thyme
½ cup oil

Soak the tomato slices in buttermilk while mixing the cornmeal, flour and spices together. Dredge the tomato slices in the cornmeal mixture while the oil is heating in a skillet. Sauté over medium heat for about two minutes per side or until golden. Drain on absorbent towels and serve immediately.

CORN PUDDING

2 cups corn
3 cups milk
½ stick butter
3 tablespoons flour
½ cup sugar
3 eggs

Cream butter, sugar, eggs and flour. Add milk and corn. Bake at 350 degrees for 45 minutes or until firm.

PERSIMMON PUDDING

2 cups persimmon pulp
1½ cups sugar
3 eggs, slightly beaten
2 cups self-rising flour
½ teaspoon cinnamon
1 ⅔ cups milk
¼ cup butter
1 teaspoon vanilla

Mix pulp and sugar. Add slightly beaten eggs. Stir in flour with cinnamon added. Add milk and mix. Blend in vanilla and melted butter. Bake in long baking dish, buttered, at 325 degrees for 1 hour.

Bibliography

Bedini, Silvio A. "History Corner: John Vogler (1783–1881) Silversmith of Old Salem." *Professional Surveyor Magazine*, January 2001.

Begos, Kevin. "Lifting the Curtin on a Shameful Era." http://extras.journalnow.com/againsttheirwill/parts/one/storybody1.html.

Brownlee, Fambrough L. *Winston-Salem: A Pictorial History.* Norfolk, Virginia: Donning Company/Publishers.

City of Winston-Salem. Directing Board, 1940—1949; 1950–1959.

———. Government Meeting Notes. 1913–1919.

———. Government Meetings Notes, Town of Winston, 1900–1906.

———.

Dispatch. "All Over the State." November 8, 1905; August 15, 1906; June 17, 1908; August 31, 1910; September 19, 1912.

———. "Another Man Escapes in Reedy Creek Raid—Still Cut Up." August 22, 1921.

———. "Auto Owner Liable for Damage Done by Driver." October 28, 1919.

———. "A Big Revenue Raid in Stokes." August 9, 1899.

———. "County Boys Charged With Robbery, Bone $2,000 Each." January 26, 1949.

———. "Further Details About the Hail Storm." June 3, 1903.

———. "General Items." March 14, 1900.

———. "He Squealed on Daddy." August 20, 1919.

———. "Homicide at Salem." February 24, 1904.

———. "Items of Interest of Passing Events in the State of North Carolina." November 8, 1905.

———. "It Has Made My Little Boy Spry as a Rabbit." November 21, 1917.

———. "Landslide Causes Death of Workmen in the Salem Creek Valley Near Winston-Salem." November 17, 1909.

———. "Local Man Fined at Winston-Salem." September 11, 1941.

———. "Man Sent to State Prison Escaped in 1887, Recaptured in Winston-Salem after 20 Years." August 14, 1907.

———. "Mauled Winston-Salem Girl Hovers Near Death." June 17, 1950.

———. "Negro Admits He Assaulted Girl in Winston-Salem." June 25, 1950.

———. "News of North Carolina Gathered from Murphy to Manteo and Condensed for Busy Readers." October 24, 1906.

———. "Nine Hurt in Auto Wreck." June 12, 1918.

———. "Open Letter." October 5, 1898.

———. "Relative Order Is Established in Winston-Salem." November 4, 1967.

———. "Robbers Held at Winston-Salem Are Wanted Here." December 19, 1921.

———. "Stokes Sheriff Fined $50 for Being Drunk." September 10, 1921.

———. "They Ran Away." January 30, 1895.

———. "Tobacco Thieves Have Been Active at Winston-Salem." December 12, 1927.

———. "Twin City Woman Freed on Charge of Larceny Here." June 7, 1945.

———. "Two Sentenced to Death." August 11, 1915.

———. "Weird Friday Night." November 4, 1967.

———. "Winston-Salem Couple Held for Poisoning Girls." May 24, 1928.

———. "Winston-Salem Negro Is Held on Fraud Charge." September 15, 1950.

Eller, Ernest McNeill. *Salem: Star and Dawn.* N.p.: Jarboe Printing Company, 2011.

"Hotel Zinzendorg Fire: A Thanksgiving Day Disaster." http://ncpedia.org/history/cw-1900/zinzendorg.

Hoyt, William K. "The Lot, the Youth and the Schobers." In *The Three Forks of Muddy Creek.* Edited by Frances Griffin. Winston-Salem, NC: Old Salem Incorporated, 1974.

Hunter, Rixie. *The Checker Board Corridor.* Winston-Salem, NC: J.F. Blair, 1968.

James, Hunter. "A Tavern in the Town." In *The Three Forks of Muddy Creek.* Edited by Frances Griffin. Vol. 4. Winston-Salem, NC: Old Salem Incorporated, 1977.

Kevles, Daniel J. *In the Name of Eugenics.* N.p.: University of California Press, 1985.

Machlin, Milt. *Libby.* New York: Tower Books, 1980.

New York Times. "Southern Raceriot [*sic*] Costs Five Lives." November 18, 1918.

Niven, Penelope, and Cornelia Wright. *Old Salem: The Official Guidebook.* Winston-Salem, NC: Old Salem, Inc., 2000.

Reynolds, Patrick, and Tom Shachtmen. *The Gilded Leaf.* Boston: Little, Brown and Company, 1989.

Schnakenberg, Heidi: *Kid Carolina—R.J. Reynolds Jr.: A Tobacco Fortune, and the Mysterious Death of a Southern Icon.* New York: Center Street, 2010.

Shirley, Michael. *From Congregation Town to Industrial City: Culture and Social Change in a Southern Community.* New York: New York University Press, 1994.

Tursi, Frank V. *Winston-Salem: A History.* Winston-Salem, NC: John F. Blair, Publisher, 1994.

Waltz, Bob. "Remembering the Old Songs: Poor Ellen Smith." *Inside Bluegrass* (August 2002) http://www.lizlyle.lofgrens.org/RmOlSngs/RTOS-PoorEllenSmith.html.

Wikipedia. "Kathryn Grayson." http://en.wikipedia.org/wiki/Kathryn_Grayson (accessed April 21, 2011).

———. "Poor Ellen Smith." http://en.wikipedia.org/wiki/Poor Ellen_Smith.

Wiley, Mary C. "Glimpses of Small-Town Winston." In *Forsyth, a County on the March.* Chapel Hill: The University of North Carolina Press, 1949.

About the Author

Alice E. Sink is the published author of numerous nonfiction and fiction books, short stories, articles and essays. She earned her master's of fine arts in creative writing from the University of North Carolina–Greensboro. For thirty years, she taught writing courses at High Point University in High Point, North Carolina, where she received the Meredith Clark Slane Distinguished Teaching/Service Award in 2002. The North Carolina Arts Council and the partnering arts councils of the Central Piedmont Regional Artists Hub Program awarded Sink a 2007 grant to promote her writing. She lives in Kernersville, North Carolina, with her husband, Tom, and their rescued dogs and cats.

Visit us at
www.historypress.net